I0360785

"Professionals can guide care but they provide only a fraction of the effort involved in working with patients. Hospice has long recognized the importance of the family and volunteers in providing care to patients facing life-limiting illnesses. We are delighted that those integral parts of the health care system are receiving increased recognition and more attention is being paid to their role and to their needs. *Stuck in the Middle* promises to be an excellent resource for individuals who have to shoulder this burden."

J. Donald Schumacher, Psy.D.
President, National Hospice Foundation

"The consequences of long-term caregiving may be long lasting. The needs of caregivers warrant greater attention both in research and in practice."

Dr. Janice Kiecolt-Glaser
Institute for Behavioral Medicine Research
The Ohio State University

"Caregiving is one of the critical issues of our time. With the growing elderly population and rising medical costs, it is important to have a plan in place to look after our parents and loved ones. *Stuck in the Middle,* not only examines the problems with current care giving, but also provides solutions and tips for caregivers and those seeking to help friends and relatives."

Millard Fuller, Founder
Habitat for Humanity International

"Barbara and Darby are right on target for the present struggle of balancing career and family responsibilities. They know this is not going away soon and address the difficulty head on. You can be sure this work will go to the core of one of the domestic concerns of our day. And it will provide wisdom and much needed solace."

Jerry L. Schmalenberger
Retired President,
Pacific Lutheran Theological Seminary, Berkeley, California
ELCA Global Mission Volunteer, Affiliate Faculty
Lutheran Theological Seminary, Hong Kong

"*Stuck in the Middle* addresses a subject that is near and dear to my heart, and to my exhausted spirit. It gives me great comfort to know that I'm not the only one dealing with this amazing honor.....this tremendous responsibility...... this mind-boggling job. God bless Barbara and Darby for sharing their stories and their spirit-reviving tips."

Karen Taylor-Good
Grammy-nominated songwriter
Two time SESAC Songwriter of the Year

The engaging and touching stories in Stuck in the Middle make you feel you are not alone. The stories lovingly get you unstuck from the wrenching emotions and stresses of a parent aging and dying. It's a great Rx for not only dealing with it but also growing from the experience.

Michael Brickey, Ph.D.
America's Anti-Aging Psychologist and author of *Defy Aging*

Being a downsizing specialist and working with clients who have the responsibility to take care of their parents and their children, we see first hand how overwhelming the entire process is. This trend is directly affecting the Baby Boomer generation and *Stuck in the Middle* addresses everything someone needs to know on how to get through it. It will be a great resource for our clients.

Janine E. Aquino, President
Estate Group of Ohio, Ltd.

As our loved ones grow older, it is very difficult for them to give up that which is comfortable and familiar even when it is time for them to do so. It is just as difficult for their children to help them make the critical decisions that will help determine their quality of life in their remaining years. *Stuck in the Middle* will be a real help in understanding the issues and some practical ways to deal with them. I only wish it had been available to me several years ago when I traveled the path of care-giver to a dear aunt as she struggled with the ageing process.

Wesley W. Mayer, President
Expert Insight, LLC

Few individuals have the patience to get through the maze of issues surrounding caretaking the elderly. *Stuck in the Middle* provides the type of solutions for others in order that they can be successful with their efforts. Thank you, Barbara, for sharing the lessons you learned.

Robert E Donald, President
The Donald Group

Stuck in the Middle

Shared Stories And Tips For Caregiving Your Elderly Parents

Barbara McVicker and Darby McVicker Puglielli

Stories written by Jim Berg and Elisa Bernick

authorHOUSE®

AuthorHouse™
1663 Liberty Drive, Suite 200
Bloomington, IN 47403
www.authorhouse.com
Phone: 1-800-839-8640

First published by AuthorHouse 2/18/2008

ISBN: 978-1-4343-3968-3 (sc)

Library of Congress Control Number: 2007907630

Printed in the United States of America
Bloomington, Indiana

This book is printed on acid-free paper.

Contents

Acknowledgments

I want to thank my writers, Jim Berg and Elisa Bernick, who transformed heart-wrenching, taped interviews into lovely stories. Jim is an award-winning screenplay writer and Elisa is author of *The Family Sabbatical Handbook: the Budget Guide to Living Abroad with Your Children*. Beth Freeman is my speaking manager. Sally Robinson created the logo. Karen Taylor-Good allowed me to use her wonderful and poignant lyrics. My daughter, Darby McVicker Puglielli, was my editor and assistant. She kept reminding me that people needed this book. My webmaster, layout designer and son, Ryan McVicker, kept me laughing when I was too tired to keep writing. My husband, Robert McVicker, supported me financially and emotionally when I quit my job as a development director in order to care for my parents full-time.

I am fortunate to have connections with nationally-known physicians and lawyers. The following provided advice:

Michael Brickey, Ph.D. author of *Defy Aging*

Geoffrey B. Blossom, MD

Donald J. Vincent, MD, FACP, professor emeritus,
　　The Ohio State Medical School

Sharon L. R. Miller, Attorney, Master of Laws of Taxation,
　　OSBA Board Certified Specialist in Estate Planning,
　　Trust and Probate Law

A very special thanks to all the people who shared their personal stories with me. I now share a few with you in this book.

Introduction

After more than 10 years of taking care of both of my parents, I know the loneliness, guilt, anger, and sorrow of caregiving. They both died at age 91. Even after all those years of caregiving, I always felt I was unprepared for the next crisis as they aged. They never did anything in a proactive manner. Everything was a conflict. I really wanted to map out a plan for them – housing, financial and medical – but they only got angry with me.

My greatest fear was that after being a caregiver, I would not have learned a thing. Not grown at all. Not figured out how to age in a positive manner. And that I would repeat the same action with my children. It would be so sad if my children gave a sigh of relief at my funeral.

Stuck in the Middle started as a list of things I would do as I aged so I would not make life difficult for my children. The list on my computer was titled "I'll be damned if I'll do this to MY children!" After I had written "The List", I signed it and had it notarized. When I age and become stubborn, mean, and demented, my kids can put this list under my nose to remind me of my previous commitment to them. I share this list with you at the end of the book.

One of the items on my list is to believe that when my kids make suggestions to me in my elder years, they will do so out of love and I should listen. When my adult children tell me it is time to move or stop driving, I am going to comply with a smile!

People started requesting the list I had written for my kids. They asked me to speak at their organizations and businesses. I became the guru of caregiving information. Soon I was giving TV and radio interviews and speaking nationally. Audiences were relieved to hear that their situations and emotions were normal. It amazed me how universal the conflicts were between the elderly and their adult children. They all felt blindsided, concerned and frustrated, just like I had felt. I started documenting my own experiences and those of others. After hundreds of interviews with caregivers and health care professionals, these notes and interviews evolved into this book.

The title of the book, *Stuck in the Middle*, came from the uneasy sense that I was truly STUCK – "stuck" caring for my children and caring for my parents while trying to manage the load of a full-time job. "Stuck" at the doctor's office with my mom when I needed to be driving the carpool to soccer or meeting a deadline on a grant proposal at work. I never dreamed I would be caring for my parents almost as long as I had taken care of my own children. I clearly remember changing my mother's diaper on a cold January afternoon, then turning to change the diaper on my grandson. Truly, STUCK in the MIDDLE!

My wish is that this book will help you and your elderly parents have a plan of action. By sharing these true life-stories with your family, hopefully a dialogue can be started that addresses the emotions and conflicts that occur during the transition ahead.

The Great Untold Secret
Barbara's Story

I know you're watching over them, I'm not in it by myself
But it's taking all the faith I have, I need some extra help
Mom and Dad are awfully frail, and getting more confused
My 15-year-old knows it all, and hasn't got a clue
And me there in the middle, both sides leaning hard
They need all my energy, I need a stronger heart

Who made me the grown up?
I don't know which scares me more
Watching Dad behind the wheel
Or my child head out the door

Give me strength, help me be the rock
Give me patience, 'cause they've all become my flock
Give me courage, as they change please help me know
You'll give me the strength to hold them
And the strength…to let them go

"Me There in the Middle"
by Karen Taylor-Good and Lisa Silver

The Great Untold Secret

I spent ten years caring for my parents. It was a stressful and frustrating ten years. Caring for them was a much harder job than raising my two children. Much, much harder. But nobody ever talks about that. Nobody prepares you for what's ahead with your parents. You go along believing that once your kids head off to college you are free and your life becomes your own again. But it is not true. The great untold secret is that the next step in life is caring for your parents and it can be a terribly difficult and lonely journey. Nobody talks about how combative they can become. Or how abusive. My parents resented losing their independence and were scared by their declining health, so they took out all their fears and concerns on me. They yelled at me, humiliated me and never once thanked me for all the work I did on their behalf. I am not saying that my parents were abusive twenty-four hours a day, but they were not warm and fuzzy people. And caring for them was not a warm and fuzzy experience.

Looking at my mom, you would never have guessed what a demanding person she was. Physically she was tiny: maybe five feet tall in heels with dainty, almost child-like features. But her small size did not diminish the power she had over my older sister and me. She taught first grade for 32 years and at home she ran a very tight ship. She allowed very little "down time" in our lives. We did not get to lie around the living room and listen to music or watch TV. We did not hang out with friends. We learned how to play instruments, went to dance class and prepared for the debate team. There was a lot of pressure to excel and bring home blue ribbons and gold trophies. My sister did fine, but I never felt like I measured up to my mom's exacting and rigid standards. In some ways, life at home was really hard. But it was also a place of learning and activity, and that was really wonderful.

My father was a passive-aggressive alcoholic his entire life. He was not a nice person. He was cruel and distant and I often felt afraid of him. Looking back, I think my mom was trying to keep us busy to keep us out of reach of my dad's miserable moods. He had a special chair in the living room that nobody else was allowed to sit in. It was a big, gray, overstuffed rocking chair next to a little side table where he set his drink. Even when he wasn't sitting in it, that big gray chair looked just like my dad. Stern. Vast. Aloof.

I remember one Saturday night my father was arrested for drunk driving and it made the headlines in the newspaper the next day. The article identified everyone in my family by name and all the horrible details of his arrest. That Sunday morning we had to walk into church as if nothing had happened. My sister and I had to walk down the church aisle between our parents pretending my father hadn't been arrested the night before. Total hypocrisy.

My parents had a terrible relationship with each other. It was basically open warfare. I remember lying in bed each night trying not to cry as I listened to my parents fight downstairs. Their abusive words wafted up through the heat registers like some kind of poisonous gas. It went on like that for years. And when my sister and I moved out of the house, my parents' relationship with each other got even worse.

In 1993, I started taking care of them. They needed help and I knew I had to do it, but caretaking for them did not come with a lot of love; it came with a lot of duty. Every day I dealt with two adults who were acting like toddlers fighting over the same toy. Not only was I trying to help them make choices and move through transitions, I had to deal with how poorly they worked together and all of their dysfunctional past history.

The caretaking part started when they were still in their own home. I tried to get over there every day to make sure certain things were happening. I was responsible for paying their bills, maintaining their property, and mopping up the crises they would get into. I tried to have my cleaning lady clean their house but she did not do "a good enough job" for my mother. I tried to hire out lawn mowing but the person "did not do it the way we like it." It was very difficult to bring in anybody who was up to my parents' standards. Like many older people, they did not like having strangers in their house. So guess who got to clean their house and mow their lawn each week? Me.

My mother was a severe diabetic and never ate properly to keep her diabetes under control. She lived her day however she wanted and then suffered the health consequences, which were sometimes serious. My dad was physically and mentally fine, but he refused to help me in anyway. That's the way he was. Cantankerous. I would ask him to make sure mom ate lunch and he would say, "I can't." Which meant, "I won't." He really did not do much except watch TV all day. It went on like that for a few years until my mother's health and my father's mental abilities deteriorated to the point where I had to take some action.

The crisis that moved my parents from their home into a retirement center was, unfortunately, a pretty common one. My dad's judgment became so impaired that he sent $68,000 in cashier's checks to Canada after he received a long distance telephone call telling him he had won the Canadian lottery. "All you need to do," the caller told him, "is send $98,000 to cover the taxes on your prize and we'll send you a check for one million dollars."

I had told my parents over and over about telephone scams. In fact, I had gotten them an answering machine and told them if they did not recognize the voice, they weren't supposed to even pick up the phone. When I did my daily visits, I made sure to listen to all the messages that had been left to see if there was anything important they had missed.

I thought I had set up a system to ensure their safety, but obviously it did not work. My dad thought he was being so crafty and clever about the lottery scam that he sent the money without anyone's knowledge. I only found out about it when his bank called me one morning, just as we were heading out of town for a week's vacation. "Your dad has requested a cashier's check for quite a large some of money," the banker told me. "It is his third one in two weeks and this one is for $30,000. Is that OK?" I had no idea what she was talking about. "Keep him there," I told the banker. "Don't let him leave. I'm on my way." When I got to the bank, we called in the FBI who said the Canadian lottery story was a very common scam. By then, my father had already sent away $68,000 and his name was on every scam artist's list around the country.

I spent the next 24 hours frantically shutting down every financial account that had my parents' names associated with it so that nobody could get their hands on any more money. My family was supposed to have already left for our vacation and we delayed it so I could close down all those accounts: stocks, social security, everything. A big part of caregiving for someone else is constantly being faced with dilemmas and decisions and having to choose one thing over another. Do we cancel our vacation to deal with this crisis? Who are more important: my nuclear family or my parents? We ultimately decided to go on vacation because the kids and my husband were so looking forward to it, but I remember crying the whole eight-hour ride to our lake house. I actually cried the entire vacation. I was crying out of anger and out of fear of what would happen next. My life had already been so altered by caring for my parents and I knew it would just be even more affected as time went on. I think I was already so tired that it was hard for me to see how I was going to find the energy for the years ahead. I also felt very much alone. None of my friends at the time were going through this. My husband was busy with work. I did not have anyone to talk to. And who can you talk to about it? People say, "Why don't you go to a support group?" Oh sure, at 10:00 at night with my floppy slippers on? Where do you go at that time of night?

At the time, I was furious with my father. But looking back it was probably a good thing it happened. It was a lot of money to lose, but nobody got hurt physically, and ultimately it got my parents to move out of their house. They did not move out gracefully of course. My dad refused to visit any of the facilities I had researched, so my mom chose where they would move. Both of them moved out of their home with a sour "I'll show you" kind of attitude.

But the good thing was that everything that happened after the move happened in baby steps. I'm talking about the decline in their physical and mental health. I can not imagine how people cope when somebody dies suddenly while still in their house and the adult children have to mourn a loved one while coping with all the legal and financial details of their life. All the work that's required is so overwhelming including dealing with material possessions and bill collectors. In my parent's case, I was able to be methodical and downsize gradually because I became the trustee of all their accounts. I still had to deal with all of their possessions and the legal and financial details of their lives, but at least I could do it while they were living in a retirement center.

I'm not sure whether it is Depression Era thinking or just a lack of energy for cleaning things out, but I think most elderly people hoard stuff. They end up with a house full of junk. My parents had boxes and boxes of Christmas decorations from 1923 and enough toilet paper to cover the needs of everyone in town. And I couldn't just toss it all out; there was buried treasure amidst all the junk: rare coins and stock certificates, ten and fifty dollar bills, and reams of lovely writing. I tried to have my parents help me sort through things while they were still living in the house but that did not work very well. Having them there in the clutter trying to sort through the flotsam and jetsam of their lives was way too hard on them mentally and emotionally. It was frustrating for me as well because nothing ever got done. It was better that I went through it once they moved out. Then I could put the house on the market and clear the decks.

My parents first moved into the independent living section of a lovely retirement center. I had decorated the apartment with some of their favorite things from their house so the moment they walked in it felt like home. Walking into an unfamiliar apartment filled with boxes would have been too difficult emotionally, but doing it this way worked out well. To be able to move into the independent living part of the facility, my parents had to prove they could handle specific safety issues as well as their own health concerns, dressing and cooking.

When my parents moved into the retirement center, they decided they were going to be miserable and they were. There were so many activities and opportunities available to them, but instead they decided to complain about everything and everybody. They were miserable during their first four years there and I showed up every day to hear about it.

As my mom's health deteriorated both physically and mentally, she became even less able to manage her diabetes. I eventually hired a nurse to supervise her breakfast in the morning. I would go in at noon to make sure she ate lunch, and I hired an aide to go in at dinnertime. We limped along like that for awhile but even then sometimes she would crash. Her diabetes would overwhelm her and the nurses from the nursing part of the facility would have to rush over to care for her. Eventually, the facility administrators told us they couldn't keep providing staff to run over to help my mom and it was time for her to move into assisted living.

I had absolutely no idea how I was going to get my mom to move into assisted living. She was a very stubborn person, and once people are in independent living, they often dig in and refuse to move to another section of the facility. My mother's attitude was, "Don't you *ever* put me in *there*." I really did not know what I was going to do. Ultimately, I got a lucky break and my mom got very sick and was admitted to the hospital. I know that sounds horrible, but she was in the hospital long enough to forget about what her life had been like before. When she got well again, I was able to move her straight from the hospital into assisted living. I can honestly tell you that assisted living was the best thing that happened to my mom in the last ten years of her life.

The positive social aspects of assisted living were incredible. My mother made a best friend which she had very few of in her life. She and

Lucille would sit together and hold each other's hands and eat at the table together. They would brush each other's hair and tell each other secrets. It was very sweet. And there were so many other human interactions there as well. Even though I visited every day, I couldn't make my mother stretch mentally and physically like the staff did. They made her talk to people all day long. There was very little turnover in staff there and they all knew her and had a history with her. She went to exercise class and played cards and she laughed and giggled and the best part was I got to do all of that with her.

Until then, I couldn't even consider *enjoying* time with my mother because all I could handle was caretaking for her. But with the caretaking left to someone else, I could truly enjoy time with my mom. It was a wonderful three years for her in assisted living. It may sound strange, but the last two years in particular were wonderful because my mom had vascular dementia due to her diabetes and other health problems. She was like a two-year-old in terms of being able to live in the moment. All her anger and past frustrations disappeared with her memory. And by then my dad had died, so he wasn't a frustration to her either. Just like with a two-year-old, I was able to coax her out of an unhappy mood by distracting her with something new. And because of that she really enjoyed her days. If she were pouting over something I would say, "It is a beautiful day, Mom. Let's go for a walk." She would look out the window and immediately forget all her worries. "Oh, yes," she would say. "It is sunny today. Let's go." I had more fun with my mom in those last two years than I ever had. We laughed and giggled, and let me tell you something, my mom wasn't normally a giggler. And there were even a few times she said to me, "What would I ever do without you?" Before this time, there were very few moments when I felt like she thought I was a good daughter. My mother and I had a really nice relationship at the end.

Unfortunately, when my mom was moved to assisted living, things did not go at all well for my dad. He started calling me at 3 a.m. each morning to complain and worry. He was getting more and more confused and he really went downhill quickly. He was still living alone and he did not quite understand why my mom was in assisted living and he was still in independent living. He wasn't supposed to take meals with her but he would just sort of hang around until he actually started to become a problem for the staff. And then one day he fell and they sent him to the emergency room.

Caretaking is a long and exhausting process. And you really do feel stuck between caring for your parents and taking care of everything else in your life. When I got the call that my dad was in the emergency room, my adult son was also in the hospital. Where do you go? Who has priority? Trying to juggle family, house, job and all the emotional aspects of the situation is almost impossible. I ended up visiting both my son and my father at two different hospitals.

They released my dad from the emergency room directly into the nursing home and, I'll be honest, he was essentially just warehoused there until he died. He went in walking and talking, but he quit doing both almost immediately and he died within six months. When he first went into the nursing home, it was actually rather nice because I could bring my mom over to see my dad, we would sit with him for awhile, and then I would go back with my mom and eat with her. If he had been in a hospital during that period, it would have been much harder for me to care for them both.

Frankly, I did not have many feelings for my dad at this point. I had finally given up on the idea of reconciliation with my father, something I held on to for many years. He had yelled at me, humiliated me and put me down so much by then that all I really felt for him in the end was indifference. My dad never said thank you, he never looked happy to see me or laughed or expressed any kind of positive emotion towards me. But I accepted him for who he was and accepted the indifference I felt for him. It was all I could do.

One Friday night about ten o'clock, I had just put my mom to bed upstairs in assisted living, and I came back down to the nursing home to say one more goodnight to my dad. In the few minutes my mom and I had been gone, he had died. I felt okay about it. I had spent many, many hours with him before he died and I felt peaceful with his death. I did not love him or hate him or really feel much of any emotion. But I did feel peaceful when he died and that was enough.

For two years afterwards, my mother remained relatively healthy and happy until the night I got a phone call that she had fallen. I went to the emergency room and found her fractured all to pieces. She was literally in pieces. The worst thing was she had fractured her pelvis and a pelvis can't be set, it has to heal itself. She was a 91-year-old woman with osteoporosis and severe diabetes lying on a hospital bed in terrible agony. They did surgery on her hips but they could not do anything for her pelvis. She was in so much pain and so confused she did not even know she was in the hospital. She did not understand why everyone was hurting her so badly.

I asked the doctors whether she was going to get better. I asked them if she would ever truly heal and be pain-free, and they told me they honestly did not know. At that moment, I knew I was facing a very hard decision. I believe there is a point when you decide to help a person get better if it is possible, but if it isn't possible you need to decide to help a person die peacefully. After a lot of thought, I decided to help her die with dignity.

They moved my mother to the palliative care wing of the hospital until my sister and other relatives could fly in, and then they moved her into the hospice area where she spent the last three days of her life. The hospice people were wonderful.

Even though I think the decision to help her die was the right one, I have gone back and revisited that decision again and again. It is a hard decision to make. But given the pain she was in and how remote the possibility was that she would ever escape that pain, I believe it was the right decision.

My mom was pretty lucid right up to the end. For awhile, I thought about asking her whether she was ready to die and how was she feeling about it, but I did not ask her either question. I did not want her worrying about what was ahead of her, and I was not sure she knew she was going to die. But maybe she did, because she stopped eating and her body started to shut down. We bumped the drugs up so she wouldn't feel any pain and, at the end, we gave her a drug to slow down her breathing and keep her comfortable as she slipped away. It was a very humane ending. We had already done so many interventions. This seemed to be the natural course of things, and it was time to say enough is enough.

Both my mom and dad had relatively peaceful endings, and, generally speaking, the end was peaceful for me as well. But the journey to the end with my parents was anything but peaceful. It felt like slogging through a swamp with logs tied to my ankles. Caregiving for parents is a lot like caregiving for babies, but without any of the positives attached. There are no thank-you's or smiles from the general public for what you're doing. Nobody comes up to you on the street and coos at your parents or pats you on the back. It is your own personal drama and society does not acknowledge your burden. And even though many of the physical responsibilities are the same, caring for elderly people is not at all like caring for babies. Old people aren't cute. They won't necessarily be any better tomorrow or more verbal or more cheerful or want to learn something new. Often they are in diapers again and completely dependent on you, which feels humiliating to both you and your parents. It just is not easy. But it also does not have to be a big, uncomfortable secret. It is waiting for all of us down the road. Maybe if we acknowledge it with each other, and give each other more encouragement and support, we can unhook the logs from around our ankles and feel lighter and more peaceful as our parents take their last few steps and wave their final good-byes.

The Caregiver...
Survival, Challenges, Rewards

———— ⌒ ————

Survival

Consider your own needs: put your oxygen mask on first

Accept help

Realize limits and set boundaries

Expect setbacks

Take time off

Stay healthy: eat and sleep

Normal, common feelings: anger, resentment, guilt, inadequacy, loneliness, grief

Information is empowering: research through books, doctors, social workers, internet

Plan something to look forward to (fun outing, vacation, etc.)

Plan your day so you can have a respite

Have a mentor: connect with someone who has been a successful caregiver

Join a support group

Be prepared to say "goodbye"

Live one day at a time

Be proactive

Let go of futile efforts

Examine your motivation for caregiving

Don't sacrifice yourself for the perceived good of your parents without including your own need. If you try to remain a full-time caregiver without caring for yourself, you will burn-out or become ill yourself.

Challenges
Symptoms of Caregiver Burn-out
Denial: "I know Dad will get better"

Anger: due to not setting boundaries, doing more than you can handle

Social Withdrawal: from friends and activities, due to less time for self, feeling alone

Anxiety: about the future

Guilt: for not rescuing parents from the pain and loneliness of old age, for not meeting siblings' expectation about caregiving, conflicting "shoulds"

Depression: lost ability to cope with the aging parent, no laughter

Exhaustion: physically and emotionally tired

Sleeplessness: too many concerns and tasks, fatigue

Irritability: moodiness, overwhelmed

Lack of Concentration: "Caregiver Attention Deficit Disorder"

Health Problems: never feel well, headaches

Financial and legal burdens: college tuition, retirement, and nursing home for parents

Competing demands: career, children, aging parents

Questions to ask yourself:
Do you feel that your parent asks for more help than she needs?

Do you feel that because of the time you spend with your parent you do not have time for yourself?

Do you feel stress between caring for your parent and caring for your own family/job?

Do you feel angry when you are around your parent?

Do you frequently feel burdened caring for your parent?

Does caring for your aging parent make you feel badly about yourself?

Are there options you are not considering because of things you promised years ago that are no longer feasible? Example: "Never put me in a nursing home!"

> If you answered yes to several of the above questions,
> you are experiencing burn out
> and should seek help from relatives and/or professionals.

The Psychology of the Past

The caregiving stage of life includes balancing attachment and separation. It also puts the entire family under stress, to the point where even the "best" family has conflict and hurt feelings. This often manifests itself in the primary caregiver being pushed, burdened, hated, and manipulated by parents, siblings, and other family members.

The more difficult the childhood relationships with your parents, the less likely you are to firmly separate from them. Many times the adult child regresses back to the old parental relationship. Power struggles can be a reaction to loss and/or role reversal. The adult child now has power over the difficult parent, thus there may be abuse. Anger at the parent may be a reaction to the present or something from the past.

It is time to mourn that you did not have a perfect family, and now, never will.

Rewards!

A sense of purpose, meaning, and satisfaction

Ability to value the present: being in each moment

Fulfillment of lifelong commitment, faithfulness to parent

Opportunity to give back to aging parent

Religious experience: Biblical to "honor thy parents"

Opportunity to right past wrongs

Chance to reconnect with relatives

Opportunity to love unconditionally without expectation or reward

Chance for the caregiver to demonstrate his best

Transformational

Grace: chance to break the cycle of dysfunction

The Queen Says Goodbye

Gretchen's Story

How can I help you say goodbye?
It's OK to hurt and it's OK to cry
Come let me hold you and I will try
How can I help you to say goodbye?

Sitting with Mama, alone in her bedroom
She opened her eyes and then squeezed my hand
She said, I have to go now, my time here is over
And with her final words she tried to help me understand
Mama whispered softly, time will ease your pain
Life's about changing, nothing ever stays the same and she said

How can I help you to say goodbye?
It's OK to hurt and it's OK to cry
Come let me hold you and I will try
How can I help you to say goodbye?

"How Can I Help You Say Goodbye?"
By Karen Taylor-Good and Burton Banks Collins

The Queen Says Goodbye

My mother was one of those people who always had everything done for her precisely the way she wanted. My sister and I grew up calling her "The Queen." She had such a commanding presence that you simply didn't refuse one of her requests. She actually looked like a queen with gorgeous clothes, wonderful jewels and, over the years, three devoted husbands who cared for her completely. But at the end of her life when the husbands had all died, The Queen's care fell to me.

My real father died of an embolism when I was eleven and my mother remarried his business partner who was a great father to me as I grew up. Years later, after my stepfather died, my mother remarried again. Her third husband, Fred, was a very nice man but he died of a massive heart attack not long after my mother married him.

For many years my mother had spent summers at her condo in Washington and winters living down here in Florida. When Fred died about 10 years ago, my mother hired a woman in Washington to clean her condo and run errands for her because my mother never ran errands for herself. If she needed medicine, someone went and got it for her. If she needed something at the store, someone ran and got it even though she was perfectly capable of doing it herself. The sad thing was, the more she refused to do these things for herself, the more she became physically unable to do anything at all.

My mother was a serious hypochondriac. She constantly went to doctors and called 911 for imaginary ailments. An emergency room nurse called me long distance from a Washington hospital one Saturday to rant at me because my mother was tying up staff there. But what could I do? That was just so like my mother. She was always dying of a heart attack or some fatal disease. Each winter of course, when she was living down here in Florida, I ran all her errands. I took her to the doctor, to the podiatrist, to the dentist and all the other things she had to do. My sister was as involved as she could be but she lives out west. My step-brother helped when he could, but his wife had Parkinson's and he traveled for his job so he really had his hands full. Most of her care fell to me because I lived the closest to her and had a life that made it possible.

About five years ago, it got to the point where my mother wasn't able to live in her condo alone any longer because she was unable or unwilling to do *anything* for herself. Thankfully, she agreed to move down here into an assisted living facility. She and I had visited a number of these facilities together the winter before she moved here, so I knew what she wanted. After I found her a spot, I went to Washington and went through all of her things and helped her decide what to keep and what to give away. Then I sold her condo, arranged for the movers, packed all her belongings, bought her plane ticket and drove a load of her stuff down to Florida along with the movers. By the time she got down here I was beyond exhausted.

When she moved into the assisted living facility, her health was not very good. Her esophagus was closing down and she couldn't swallow very well. She could only eat soft foods so I got a unit with a little kitchen so I could prepare her food because she refused to eat any of the food the assisted living staff prepared. If I didn't prepare her special food, she'd go into hysterics and call me at all hours. "I can't eat the food they serve here! I'm going to starve to death!" She'd eat only a very few things. I'd haul groceries over and fix food in big batches and freeze things in little containers and I'd get her special treats and fill up her freezer so she could microwave it. She was very particular. She wouldn't eat soft vegetables but she'd wolf down vegetable soup. It was enough to drive me crazy.

My mother was quite the complainer. She complained constantly about every little thing but in a sweet way. Sweet as a sledgehammer. That was her queenly style. I think she enjoyed the assisted living facility because she could call the nurses 24 hours a day. If they didn't come, she'd call and complain to me. "They aren't coming. They aren't doing this. They aren't doing that." She called me constantly and her obsession with her various health ailments got even worse. She took her blood pressure so often she wore out three blood-pressure machines in less than a year.

My mother was a master manipulator. She was such a good puppeteer that you often didn't realize you were a puppet. I think that's the reason my sister and I both got married so young. We wanted to escape from all her plotting. Growing up, my mother wasn't available either physically or emotionally. Both my real dad and my stepfather were prominent businessmen and my mom traveled with them constantly. My grandmother stayed with us most of the time and my sister and I really raised ourselves. Even when my mother was home, she was usually busy playing bridge and attending to her own needs or having someone else attend to them. Everyone followed her orders even when she wasn't around. She ran the show. There was never any doubt about that.

My mother neglected us but not in an obvious way. She always fixed our breakfast and made sure someone gave us lunch and dinner. Our clothes were clean and we never lacked for toys or money. But she never once hugged us. Never kissed us or inquired about our happiness or our fears. We were well fed and lived in a gorgeous home. I had my own car, two horses, and a speedboat. We even had a nine-hole golf course! But we were always alone. It was just my sister, my stepbrother and I. Poor little rich kids always alone except for Grandma.

When my mom got older and ended up alone, I felt like I owed it to her to take care of her. After all, she had cared for us as children or at least made sure somebody else cared for us. And she was a helpless 90-year-old woman. Not exactly helpless maybe, but I wanted to make sure she was cared for like she should be. It wasn't so much a mother/daughter thing. It was more like I wanted to do the right thing for another person who needed my help.

Anyway, after my mother had been at the assisted living facility for two years, she fell off a chair. I was writing Christmas cards when the staff called to say that she was on her way to the emergency room. I remember turning to my husband and saying, "My life is over." I really did say that because I knew what was coming. The doctors operated on her and we had only a few days to figure out what to do with her next. She couldn't go back to the assisted living facility and the hospital staff recommended what turned out to be a miserable rehab center. Later we found out she could have gone elsewhere, but at the time we didn't know what our options were. We felt rushed and rather helpless so we relied on the hospital to guide us and that was definitely a mistake.

She was hysterical at the rehab center most of the time. She called me at all hours of the day and night and I'd have to race over there. Her demands were constant. She was incontinent and because the place was huge and the aides weren't managed very well, my mother would end up lying in her soiled underpants and diapers. And of course she hated the food. She would call me at two in the morning to complain. "I'm starving," she would sob. "The food isn't soft enough. It tastes terrible. They're trying to kill me." On and on and on.

Then her esophagus totally shut down so they had to put a feeding tube in because she couldn't swallow. The feeding tube was ultimately a blessing because the whole feeding and eating thing had gotten to be a nightmare. And because she refused to do any kind of therapy for walking or to increase her strength, she was basically wheelchair bound from that point forward. She was extremely weak because she refused to do anything for herself and she couldn't do anything for herself because she was weak. It was a vicious circle.

A few months later when she had completed her rehab, I had to decide where to put her next. It was obvious she couldn't go back to the assisted living unit so I started looking for a nursing home. Finding a good nursing home was one of the toughest things of all. I talked to the licensed practical nurses (LPNs) and nurses at the hospital and rehab center to get their recommendations, but it was hard to know if they were telling me the truth. I checked the patient-nurse-aide ratios at different facilities but I don't think nursing homes tell the truth about that. I visited what seemed like a hundred places checking out how clean they were, how they smelled, and whether people were left sitting around without any attention. I looked at how many times a week the patients were bathed; I wanted it twice a week at least.

I found the aides to be the biggest problem. The pay in nursing homes is terribly inadequate and staff turnover is usually very high. The night aides in particular were pretty bad. I'd go in to check on places at night and find aides just sitting there eating pizza and ignoring the patients' beepers. Finding enough qualified staff is a huge problem everywhere. It took me a lot of time to find her a good nursing home.

But thankfully, I found my mom a great place where they had a lot of organized activities. She went to bingo several times a week and the church service each Sunday. She enjoyed those things very much. But even in a good place I had to stay on top of everything. Each time I visited, I checked mother's sheet to make sure her medications happened on time and I also looked at all the doctor's notes. I tried to be nice and honest with the staff. I didn't want to bother them too much so I took care of a lot of stuff myself. I had to balance advocating for my mom without the staff hating me. Sometimes I felt like a monster, but what else could I do? I used to write big signs in magic marker and tape them up all over her room for the staff to see. "Please leave her door open or else she gets worried." "Please leave the bathroom light on so she's not in the dark." "She requires three pillows on her bed." That sort of thing. I felt a little embarrassed doing it, but it's the only way my mom got the care she needed. Also, no matter how much the nursing home tried to prevent it, things kept getting stolen from her room and bedside table. That's just the nature of those facilities. She loved jewelry but I never kept expensive or valuable things there. I kept inexpensive costume jewelry there for her and even that would walk away at times. I also never let her clothing go to the laundry because I knew all her fine things would disappear.

I think my mother liked the nursing home but I'm not sure she really knew how to be happy anywhere by that point. What do you do when a 92-year-old woman calls you up constantly and begins sobbing? How do you comfort her? I'd say, "Mother, you're fine." "No I'm not...sob, sob." You never have any peace while caring for a parent. It's horrible. I would wake up in the middle of the night and worry that I should be doing this and that. Sometimes I wouldn't get any sleep at all.

The cost of nursing home care is astronomical. And it's even worse if you have queenly ways like my mom. She was lucky that she had enough money to cover the majority of her care. Her Medicare coverage only went for two years and by the time she died, her own money was nearly gone. She had no medication insurance and she paid $500-$1000 each month out-of-pocket for her medicine. I paid to have her hair and nails done each week. I put fresh flowers in her room because she loved flowers. I hired a care-keeper to come in every evening and get her ready for bed. This woman would sit and listen to mother complain for an hour or more each night before putting her to bed. She was wonderful and my mother loved her but she didn't come cheap. Of course the nursing home staff could have gotten my mom ready for bed but my mother wouldn't allow it. "They don't do it right," is what she always said and I wasn't going to argue with her. She went through three boxes of tissue a day. She broke one hearing aid and lost the other one so I had to buy her two new ones at a cost of $5200. It all just kept adding up. Medicare didn't pay for any of that stuff and I wasn't going to ask my husband to pay for her care. I was planning to get a job to pay for everything when her money ran out.

The nursing home was also expensive because the staff didn't want to be liable for anything. When a minor medical problem came up they immediately sent my mom to the hospital. Even if they could have easily called someone in to do a mobile x-ray or something like that, they wouldn't because they didn't have the staff to deal with the problem and they didn't want to get sued if something went wrong. There was a standing Do Not Resuscitate (DNR) order in my mom's file and they still called 911, even though my mom requested them not to.

At one point, my mom's feeding tube got infected and she developed pneumonia while we were out of town. They called us to say she was on her way to the hospital and she was dying. So I called my sister and we were quite prepared to say goodbye but when I got to the hospital, my mom was in the ICU. I asked the nurses why and they said she told them she didn't want to die. It was intervention after intervention and that's why healthcare is in such a crisis. Here was a 92-year-old woman in the hospital for a week. She had signed everything so the hospital staff could legally let her go, and instead they spent thousands and thousands of dollars keeping her alive because at the last minute she said she didn't want to die. And who can blame her?

Anyway, while I was doing all this crazy running around for my mom, paying her bills and keeping all her records, the rest of my life was falling apart. Caring for a parent takes so much time that it's easy to forget about everything else. I was at the nursing home several hours each day and I was often gone when my husband got home from work. I was exhausted all the time and depressed and it was disrupting my own life so much that I finally realized I had to change things. It essentially came down to her or me. I decided not to visit her every day, but to go every other day instead. I made this decision out of desperation. It wasn't my husband. He never complained. It was me. I was falling apart emotionally, physically, and I had to change things. On the days I didn't go, I tried not to think about her. She still called of course, and I had to deal with her bills and all that, but I did more things for myself and my family. My husband noticed the difference immediately. I was calmer and less depressed and he and my kids were delighted that I made that decision.

The guilt over not visiting her daily was initially overwhelming but ultimately it was a good decision. I didn't necessarily call her to let her know I wasn't coming, I just didn't go. My husband and I started having friends over again and it was like I picked up the pieces of my life and started it up again. Things were the same with my mom and she didn't seem to realize that I wasn't coming so often. I still did her laundry and those sorts of chores for her. And my mom had found a friend at the nursing home, which helped a lot.

Well, after about two years in the nursing home my mother caught a cold that just wouldn't go away. About three weeks before she died she said, "Gretchen, this it. I'm not going to recover from this." I said, "Mom, that's foolish talk." She'd had many colds like this over the years and she'd always recovered. And because she was such a hypochondriac, I figured it was just another one of those times.

But this time she was right. Because of that lingering respiratory infection, they couldn't give her a flu shot and on Christmas Eve night she got the flu. She'd actually gotten up and gotten herself dressed that morning, which was basically unheard of, and she'd gone to the Christmas Eve Mass they were holding there. We were there to visit in the afternoon and I remember looking at her in the wheelchair thinking, "She's an old, old woman." She was like a skeleton barely able to sit up by herself.

That night she got very sick. All the kids and grandchildren were in town and staying here at my house so I was busy Christmas Day with them, and we had two couples from out of town staying with us. The kids visited my mom on Christmas Day and she was well enough to recognize them, but when they left she got extremely sick and stayed sick. The entire next week she coughed and coughed and could not catch her breath. It just broke my heart. She would call and beg to go to the hospital. They had her on oxygen and breathing treatments and special medications to help her breathe. Really, there wasn't much more they could have done at the hospital except maybe a tracheotomy. But that probably would have killed a 93-year-old woman.

I still feel guilty because we had so much family staying with us and I couldn't get over to the nursing home as much as I wanted that week between Christmas and New Year's. New Year's Day we went out of town to visit my husband's sister and when I got back that evening, I went right over to spend a few hours with my mother. She was so bad. Coughing constantly. We met with her doctor and he was honest with

Mom that they'd tried everything they could and she was probably not going to get any better. The next morning, as I was headed out the door to go to the nursing home, the head nurse called. "Do you want to be with your mother when she dies?" That's how she put it, which I thought was horrible. The nurse said my mother was completely unresponsive. I hurried over and she died that evening. She was comatose that entire last day which was a blessing because she was so sick.

While my mom was lying there in a coma her friend came in and so did the woman who cared for her each evening. And then the basketball game came on and my mother loved basketball. She was crazy about it. So we tried to treat it as a normal day. We visited and laughed and watched the game. We included her as best we could. We weren't having a good time necessarily, but we were there with her. We held her hand and washed her face. I had brought fresh flowers along and I set them on her bedside table. I'm not sure she could smell them, but I wanted her to have all of her favorite things near her at the end.

My stepbrother is a minister and he came later that afternoon and conducted a church service in her room. I know she would have liked that a lot. And even though she was in a coma, none of us thought she was going to die so quickly. I wish I'd taken her more seriously when she told me she wasn't going to recover from that last illness. I will always regret that I didn't believe her. I'm not sure what I would have done differently but maybe I would have felt a bit more prepared for her death. I do feel that we treated her like a queen right up to the end. She died in bed with her loyal subjects gathered around her and the scent of fresh flowers drifting through the air. It was a dignified ending. As she took her last breath I thought, "The Queen is bidding the world goodbye." Maybe it's sad that I didn't think of her as my mom at the end. But in all honesty, I think she's just as happy to be remembered as "The Queen."

End of Life: Difficult Choices and Grief

For everything there is a season,
And a time for every matter under heaven:
A time to be born, and a time to die

Ecclesiastes 3:1

Humans have the distinction of being the only living thing that knows we are going to die during our whole life. We do not know when, but we know it as an inevitable part of life. Death is a natural process of life. The generations living today are the first faced with making difficult end-of-life choices. Medical advancements have changed and complicated the landscape of life and death.

How wonderful! How difficult! How sacred!

People in the process of dying say there are two things they are afraid of: being in pain and being alone. As caregivers, we can alleviate both

It is possible to be gracious and funny at the end. When Bob Hope was ill and dying, his family asked him to let them know where he wanted to be buried. He replied, "Surprise me!"

End of Life choices

As your parent approaches death, several choices need to be made. It is often helpful if these choices are made with the parent ahead of time.

These choices can be made legal by having written Advance Directives (TIPS: Medical and Legal Documents). The Advance Directives need to be readily available because health care professionals treat a patient when uncertain of his wishes. Emergency Medical Technicians (EMT's) will treat a person unless there is a Do Not Resuscitate (DNR) order at hand.

It is important to understand that some people do not benefit from cardiopulmonary resuscitation (CPR) long-term. If the patient has multiple medical problems, is not living independently, has a terminal disease, has dementia or is very elderly and frail, CPR will only prolong the dying process. The person will not achieve a greater quality of life.

End of life questions

What are the possible benefits compared with the possible risks?

Will the treatment make the patient better or merely keep him alive longer?

Is it time to keep the patient comfortable and out of pain, and thus allow a natural death?

Is the person likely to die within 6 months even if treatment is continued?

What are the wishes of the patient?

Is the goal to cure the patient, or is it time to provide comfort?

If any of the answers include the thought that it is time

to allow for a natural and comfortable death, consider Hospice.

Hospice

Hospice is a special kind of humane and compassionate care designed to provide sensitivity and support for people in the final phase of a terminal illness. Hospice care can be provided in a variety of settings: in-home, in hospital or in a nursing home. About 90% of Hospice is provided in the home. Hospice is covered by Medicare, Medicaid and most private insurance plans. Most people wish they had requested Hospice earlier. Hospice is about choice. Hospice believes that quality of life is as important as length of life. Hospice focuses on care, not cure. Patient and family are both cared for.

Physical signs of dying

Coolness

Sleeping

Disorientation

Incontinence

Congestion

Restlessness

Fluid and food intake decrease

Urine output decreases

Breathing pattern changes

Mental/spiritual signs of dying

Withdrawal

Vision-like experiences

Decreased socialization

Unusual communication

Asking permission to die

Saying good-bye

For those left behind: Stages of Grief

Denial

Anger

Bargaining

Depression

Acceptance

Experiencing the grief

...is beneficial. Accept the reality of the event, and feel the pain. Work on reordering life without that person, and begin to move on. Emotions that you feel can include disbelief, sorrow, guilt, regret, fear, anxiety, distractedness, crying or inability to cry, relief.

People grieve in different ways. Some are intuitive (feelers) and need to talk and feel the emotions. Some are instrumental (doers) and need to be busy and physical.

Reaction to your relative's death depends upon

Your age
Relationship to the person who died
Whether there was "unfinished business"
Whether the death was expected
Your past experiences with loss
How your family responds to death
Your expectations
Your belief system
Your coping skills
Whether you communicate your grief with others

Helping the grieving person:

Ask questions like:
+ What do you want?
+ What do you need?
+ What do you fear the most?

Listen
Be there for the person
Stay connected: emotionally and physically
Ask about the person who died
Tell stories about the person who died
Start a memory box

Peace Begins at Home
Joe's Story

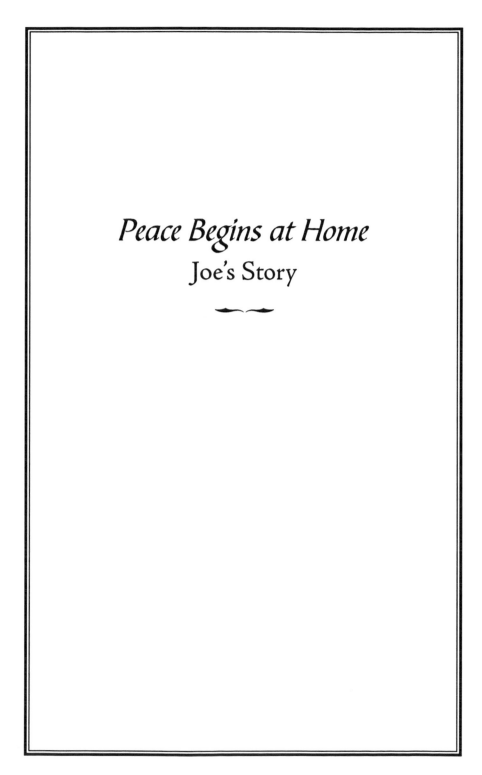

The bruises on his face will go away
Mom keeps him home from school until they fade
She's sorry he was born and tells him so
He takes it in, he hangs his chin
He ducks another blow

Did God overlook it?
What ought have been written
The Eleventh Commandment...honor thy children

Thou shalt not kill, Thou shalt not steal
Thou shalt not take the Lord's name in vain
Thou shalt not cause thy children pain

God does not overlook it...what ought have been written
The Eleventh Commandment...honor thy children
Honor thy children

"The Eleventh Commandment"
Karen Taylor-Good and Lisa Aschmann

Peace Begins at Home

I never loved my mother. She beat us, my brother and me, often when we were young. She beat me once, she said, just to toughen me up. She beat my brother one fine summer day for letting the neighbor kids play barber with him, cutting his wavy hair into unruly patches across his head. I chuckle a bit today thinking about it. She beat him for letting the neighbor kids get the best of him. That's how my mother thought.

It's difficult to describe her beatings. They weren't part of a coherent discipline regime; they weren't spankings for misbehaved children; they were quite simply beatings. My mother, her eyes wide and glassy, would lose any semblance of control. Grabbing whatever was near – a brush, a mirror, a paddle – she would start hitting us across the back, the arms, the legs, and the body. I learned to drop to the ground, blocking blows to my head with my arms and taking what blows I could with my legs. But that just made her crazier.

The beatings were common and extreme. She would accuse us of something and lose it, falling into a rage that I can't accurately describe. You had to see it. There was nothing that precipitated her behavior. No alcohol. Insecure, neurotic, and paranoid: I suppose that's as close as I can come to any explanation. Today she hides things away so others won't find them and then she forgets where she put them and thinks someone stole them. It's comical today; as a child, it was terrifying.

I always felt like the square peg in a round hole. I read insatiably as a child because my mother would leave me alone while I was reading. As I matured physically and she could no longer beat me up, her rages changed. She would lose it and stalk out of the house or she would scream and rant through the house for hours.

Then, as a young man and new father, I avoided my mother as much as possible; families, though, have a way of pulling you back. Even dysfunctional ones. I couldn't completely sever the ties. I remember her visiting once when I was a new father and she a new grandmother. I was nervous and had trouble sleeping the whole week before she showed up. When she arrived, I forced myself to hug her. A big step, hugging her, and I bit the inside of my lip until it bled.

And I have forced myself to say that I love her. I'm a believer to an extent of the "fake it, till you make it" school of thought. I scripted events in my head. Hug her, say I love her. Script them and then do them until it wasn't so unnatural. Fortunately, my wife is patient and understanding, and she has helped me immeasurably over the years. I think I knew intuitively from the beginning that she would help me in the endeavor of forgiving my family. There was always a peace and serenity to my wife and her family, and I was drawn to that. My wife has always said that we are in this together, that all of these issues are addressed as a family. That peace begins at home. She says that a lot, "Peace begins at home." God bless her.

With my wife's support and understanding, with counseling and a lot of soul-searching, I have moved beyond my anger. And, I believe, that with forgiveness – or, at least, acceptance of the past – I have reclaimed all the power and dignity that my mother took from me all those years ago. And it is absolutely essential to have worked out all the family dynamics *before* the caregiving began. I couldn't do it otherwise.

The question still remains though: Why am I a caregiver for a mother I never loved? Well, she is my mother and with that comes some responsibly. I think it is simply the right thing to do. I like to tell people a story I heard a long time ago that has helped me as I matured and agonized over my relationship with my mother. There was an old

Quaker guy who walked with a friend to work every morning in New York City. And every morning they would stop to buy the daily paper at an open-air newsstand. The proprietor of the newsstand was a surly old curmudgeon who never smiled a day in his life. Every day the old Quaker guy would smile and say, "Have a nice day." And every day the proprietor would simply grunt and grimace in response. Finally, the friend asked him why he was so nice to such a rude man. The old Quaker said that he absolutely refused to let someone else – especially such a grumpy old bugger – determine his behavior. I guess that's the way I feel about my mother.

＊～＊

My mother was living in New Jersey when it became apparent that she couldn't live by herself anymore. I was in Florida and my brother was four hours away from my mother in New England. On a visit, my brother found her at home shortly after a mini-stroke, her lip drooping and her words slurring. He rushed her to the hospital, where she experienced another mini-stroke.

At this point we should have forced my mother to sell her house and move closer to either my brother or myself. Or, at least, into some sort of assisted living in New Jersey. She steadfastly fought all our efforts, and I don't make a decision like that casually. Sometimes you can see the crisis coming but you are still powerless to do anything.

She began to diminish physically more quickly than we knew. On another of his visits, my brother found my mother with a foot swollen and blue. "Swollen the size of a football," he told me on the phone. To this day, I don't know why my mother didn't tell anyone about it earlier. My wife and I had been with my mother just two weeks before she finally complained to my brother. She was still living alone at that point and kept her wound covered with a sock and shoe. As a result, it became infected and then festered. My wife and I always took mental notes of her physical changes, in the color of her skin, for example, or sudden blotches on her skin, but never thought to examine her whole body. She has always been paranoid and distrustful, especially of doctors or anyone in positions of authority, and this is the only reason I can imagine that kept her at home, silent and in pain, with a foot the size of a football.

She was hospitalized immediately, of course, and required full-time care for months. The wound on her foot was the size of a silver dollar and it wouldn't heal properly, wouldn't close, even with medical attention. You could actually see tendons. It was obvious at this point that she could no longer live on her own and that we had to act, even if it went against her wishes. So we put her house up for sale and forced her to sell it.

While she was sick – weak with a high fever and infection, wired to an antibiotic drip and being fed intravenously – we were offered a lower price on her house than we had hoped for. My astute wife said, "Take it. She will sign right now." We took it, suspecting that my mother's willingness to sell would diminish as she recuperated. Sure enough, a week after she signed the papers, she started to feel better and began to wonder if she had made the right decision.

We have the financial means for my mother to live in assisted living, but again she steadfastly refused this option and neither my brother nor I wanted to force her. We compromised. Now, my mother spends half the year with my brother in New England and the other half with my wife and me in Florida.

I can't imagine caretaking on my own. Sometimes I think that I caregive more out of love for my brother than I do out of a sense of duty to my mother. All our decisions are made together. My brother, my wife, and I split up all the secretarial aspects of caregiving (the bill paying, the insurance and legal matters) that are quite overwhelming and stressful on their own. But, mostly, by sharing her care we are able to share the emotional toll of caregiving.

I don't believe that one person can adequately take care of an elderly person and keep their sanity. When my mother is with us, she dominates our time. It is physically and emotionally taxing. It can consume us completely. She can't cook, she can't drive – she needs help with everything. In some ways, it is not unlike caring for a small child. It is a process that wears you down and sucks the life out of you; it can isolate you from the outside world. But unlike raising a child, you don't have that sense of wonder and miracle. I truly wish I felt more tenderness towards my mother; I work hard to take care of her and give her some memorable moments. And there are some. There are some laughs. But I'm afraid that I bring her little joy. It's just not something that she knew in this life.

We are working toward the move to assisted living. We know a crisis is coming which will make it impossible for us to care for her at home, but she continues to resist the idea and I can't force her. "You're putting me away," she repeated over and over last year before an experimental one month stay in an assisted living community. And though she returned from her one-month stay more mentally alert than I've seen her for some time, she still balks at the notion of returning. In her mind's eye, she doesn't see herself as frail and helpless. She told me that those people looked too old. And once when we were watching a family video, she didn't recognize herself. "Who's that?" she asked when an old woman came into the frame. "That's you, Mom," I answered. "Oh, my," she said.

Why my mother is so against assisted living, I'm not sure. My wife believes that people of her generation, of the Depression Era, think of any assisted living as a nursing home. Or, as my mother still calls it, the "old folks' home." She can't overcome that negative stereotype. I think she also has all those images from "Sixty Minutes" of the horrible living conditions for the elderly stuck into her head: people strapped in their wheelchairs and left in a corner with drool hanging on their faces. And people of my mother's generation simply have a hard time letting go of their money. Life was tough for them; they grew up with just enough to survive and the lesson they learned was to live simply, to depend on family, and to hold on to what you have. She can't imagine wasting all her money on an 'old folks home' when she can live with her sons.

I think a part of it, too, is that unreasonableness is simply a part of the aging process. She is truly in another space mentally. My mother is convinced that people, even my brother and sister-in-law, are stealing from her. She is convinced that the doctors infected her foot. She is growing deaf and refuses to buy a decent hearing aid. Or accept a hearing aid from me. She lived by herself with a foot swollen to the size of a football without telling anyone. Truly another space.

And while it could be argued that my mother has been crazy all her life, my wife's parents, compassionate and gentle people, are also beginning to exhibit the signs of unreasonableness. Refusals to accept that perhaps they shouldn't drive, even though Grandma says, "Oh, don't let the kids in the car with Grandpa. You know how he is." Refusals to consider any living option other than their own home, which they are already having a difficult time managing on their own. Unreasonableness. A part of the aging process, it seems. My wife and I, in an effort to combat the onslaught of our own unreasonableness, have promised our daughter that we would write our decisions down on paper. We will have, in effect, a contract with our daughter. In the future, if or when we become unreasonable, perhaps a written form of our ideas will help us accept or remember what is actually best. Besides, as my wife argues, "I want a choice in assisted living arrangements. Who knows better than me what I want?"

———

I think our generation has initiated a dialog on caregiving because our parents are living longer than their parents did and our society is facing new problems, and we don't want our kids to go through some of the same difficult issues that we are facing as caregivers. Let's face it, modern medicine is amazing, but we need to start addressing the issue of living with dignity and dying with dignity. I saw a television special a few years ago and the conclusion they reached was that people aren't afraid to die; they are, however, afraid of the process. They don't want to be alone and they don't want be in pain. If we have any decency – as individuals and as a community – we should act with charity and goodwill as caregivers for the elderly. We are the next generation of elderly after all. My mother was not a good person, and she was certainly not a good mother. But even she deserves some dignity in her last days.

Vascular Events: Heart and Stroke

Heart Attack is the leading cause of death. Seek medical help immediately: Call 911!

Warning Signs:
   Chest discomfort – center of chest, pressure, squeezing, fullness
   Discomfort on other parts of upper body – arms, back, neck, jaw, stomach
   Shortness of breath
   Cold sweat, nausea, light headed

Stroke is the third leading cause of death and the leading cause of adult disability. Time is crucial because drugs need to be administered within 3 hours. Seek medical help immediately: Call 911!

Warning Signs: not all warning signs occur in every stroke
   Sudden weakness in the face, arm or leg, especially on one side of the body
   Sudden confusion or trouble speaking or understanding
   Sudden trouble seeing in one or both eyes
   Sudden trouble walking, dizziness, loss of balance or coordination
   Sudden, severe headache with no known cause

ASK a Question: Recognizing a stroke
   ASK the person to smile – look for weakness or unevenness
   ASK the person to raise both arms –look for weakness, unevenness
   ASK the person to say a simple sentence – look for mental status
   ASK the person to stick out their tongue –look to see if it goes to one side

Be Prepared:
    Know the symptoms and post them for others
    Time is crucial – note time of onset of symptoms (When did
        stroke start?)
    Keep emergency numbers and list of medications next to phone
    Keep phone on low table so that it can be reached by someone
        on the floor

Transient Ischemic Attack (TIA) is a mini-stroke with stroke-like symptoms which last a few minutes to an hour. Nearly half of people who have had a TIA do not seek medical help, which is not wise because 10-20% of people who have had a TIA will have an actual stroke in the next month and 30% will have a stroke in the future. Drug intervention can often prevent a major stroke.

Risk Factors for Vascular Events (Heart and Stroke):
    High blood pressure
    Smoking
    Lack of exercise
    High cholesterol – poor diet
    Obesity
    Diabetes
    Family history
    Male
    Age (middle-age)
    Previous Vascular Event

Little Windows
Rich's Story

You're the man who celebrates my birth
Half the reason I'm on earth
But somehow you were hidden in the shadows
I spent half a lifetime at arm's length
Saw weakness in your quiet strength
But love has finally opened up my eyes

It's so good to see you, really see you at long last
I treasure every moment now, they're going by so fast
Years of longing for a father, and you already existed
Yours is such a quiet love – I almost missed it

Thought my friends had more exciting dads
They were doctors, they were college grads
And you were selling tires down on main street
Somehow I didn't understand the caring in your calloused hands
The perfect love that waits inside your heart

All the while I was wishing for "Father Knows Best"
You were loving me so much better
And those years that I wasted lost in regret
Have turned into something so tender

"Quiet Love"
By Karen Taylor-Good and JD Martin

Little Windows

Rich grew up in rural West Virginia, a coal mining and railroad town, with two brothers and a sister. He remembers the hot sun and the dust. He remembers his mother stepping outside to snap the soot off of the laundry hanging on the clothes line whenever a steam locomotive passed by. And he remembers knowing from a very early age that family was important. Family always took care of their own.

He grew up in the kind of town that a kid with any ambition wants to escape. And escape he did. But the link to family remained, and he returned for family holidays and then for his sister's funeral. She was killed in a car accident and the image of her in the coffin in the front room of their family home is indelibly etched into Rich's memory.

The link to family remained strong. Rich got married and had three daughters of his own. Then, after retiring from a career in geology, he found his parents and an aunt in need of caregiving and reaching out to him. Unable to turn away from their needs, Rich began a new journey in his life: Caregiving. This journey lasted more than a decade and changed his life forever.

"Why did I even attempt to take care of three adults?" Rich repeated the question.

A big man, with a barrel chest, wispy gray hair, Rich rubbed his chin, then smiled warmly and proceeded to tell how much his father liked to sing. "Once in my living room," Rich said, "my father got down on a knee, held my mother's hand, and sang 'My Bonnie Lies Over the Ocean' to her." Rich paused, his raspy voice like that of an old jazz singer hanging in the air, and then he finished: "My parents got to stay together until the end, and I have memories like that. That's why I did it."

He also felt strongly that it was the right thing to do. Volunteering at a nursing home in the years before his retirement, Rich witnessed first-hand how quickly some of the residents slipped away. He remembers one elderly man in particular, who shuffled quietly through the home with his head down, as though there were no one to greet him or to return a warm smile. Rich went out of his way to talk with this man and to spend some time with him. "And gol darn it," Rich said, "his head came up and he seemed alive again. Just from talking to him."

"How did I take care of three adults at the same time? Well, that's a whole different story."

His aunt, a big-hearted woman who didn't have anywhere else to go, needed care first. She had inflammation of the central nervous system so badly that she had trouble standing. The doctors had her on massive doses of steroids and her skin would peel off, almost like a burn victim.

Rich took his aunt into his home, moving her into a vacant upstairs room. Under a doctor's supervision, he began backing her off the steroids and her skin showed signs of improvement.

At the same time, his mother, in the early stages of Alzheimer's, was failing and the physical demands of caregiving were becoming too much for his father. Soon his parents were in the upstairs room next to Rich's aunt. "Not exactly the retirement I had planned," Rich joked. "But life throws you curves and you gotta keep going. Besides, it just felt right."

◆～◆

Organization was essential to Rich's new life as a caregiver, and Rich kept to the minute of his schedule if at all possible. He rose at six a.m. and prepared for the day. He fed them, bathed them, and used jugs and jugs of lotion on their skin. Not only did the lotion keep their skin in good shape, but the mini-massage felt good and relaxed them. For twelve years this basic pattern existed. Get up. Prepare. Feed them. Bathe them. And then start all over again for lunch and dinner.

The plan always needed tweaking and adjustments, of course. It never went exactly the way it was supposed to. One night, for example, Rich woke to a tremendous commotion coming from an upstairs room. He went upstairs and found his father waving his cane and cursing in the darkness at a handful of stuffed animals. His father then waved his cane at Rich and complained: "They're making a heck of a racket. You better quiet 'em down."

And over the last few years, when both of his parents and his aunt were in diapers, Rich rose at two a.m. every morning and took each of them to the bathroom. "Otherwise," he explained, "I'd spend two hours cleaning up the mess in the morning."

While Rich's organizational skills were essential, his flexibility and creativity also helped maintain a sense of calm and serenity in the household. When his mother entered the wandering and night walking phase of Alzheimer's, he bought a hospital bed and moved her downstairs. This solved two problems: She didn't have to navigate the steep stairwell anymore and when he put the rails up she wasn't able to get out of bed and wander freely. As his father slipped into Alzheimer's and the advantages of the living room became obvious, it wasn't long before three hospital beds were lined up in the living room and all three of them were on the main floor – which truly looked more like a hospital room than a living room by this time.

To corral his mother, he also rearranged furniture in the downstairs room to make it more difficult for her to get out of the house. "And, besides," he said, "my human alarms worked great. Whenever mom took to wandering, my dad or aunt would sound the alarm. 'Effe, Effe, she's gone,' I'd hear."

"How did I maintain my sanity?"

The whole bulk of his 6' 4" frame shook as he tried to contain his laughter. "Finding humor," he said, "in even the most overwhelming situations." And he went on to explain how one morning his father had wandered across the street towards a field to meet Mary, a relative who been dead for years. When Rich caught up with him, his father absolutely refused to return to the house. His mind was set on meeting Mary. Unable to bribe or trick his father into returning to the house, Rich proceeded to tow him home – all one hundred and eighty cantankerous pounds, his arms flailing and his heels dragging on the grass and then the asphalt. When a passing neighbor waved and said, "Good morning, Rich," as though nothing unusual were happening, Rich simply nodded and smiled.

Through all these years, Rich was not only fanatical about their schedule, but he was also fanatical about a break for himself. Each day he took a break between breakfast and lunch; he hired someone to watch his parents and his aunt while he went to the gym to work out. The workouts not only cleared his head, but they helped keep him in great shape – a real plus when you are caregiving three adults who are often dead weight. And, after the work out, he allowed himself some time in the sauna. The hot moist air was truly cleansing and Rich returned home renewed each day and ready to begin again.

Family, of course, also helped. "You simply can't caregive," Rich said, "without a supportive family." His wife did all the shopping, most of the errand running, and often helped feed them. His three daughters – all of whom were young adults and living at home during the early years of caregiving – supported Rich and spent many hours with their grandparents and great-aunt. Rich's father, who had many good days during his decline, sang with them and told them stories. His daughters, in fact, learned much of the family lore from him and their great-aunt. "I know they enjoyed this time," Rich said, "and I think in the future, as they grow older, they will cherish it."

The medical community, too, was instrumental in preparing Rich for his evolving role as caregiver. Though he needed to be aggressive in seeking their help, he found that the medical community was one of his few sources of support. While everyone else was telling him that he couldn't possibly take care of three adults, the medical community supported him. Over the years, with their help, he learned all the tricks to feed someone who has lost the swallowing reflex, to bathe someone who is trying to hit you, to catheterize, to treat wounds, and how to give IV fluids and medications.

He also learned how to create the right "essence." Rich smiled, telling about a nurse from Hospice who came to offer advice in the early stages of caregiving. A real hippie, he said, like she had just stepped in from Haight-Ashbury, but there was a peacefulness and calm about her. She walked through the house thoughtfully, jotting down notes, and then she looked at Rich and said: "How about some essence?"

"What do you mean?" Rich asked. "Essence?"

"Music and aromas," she said simply. "Music and aromas."

From that afternoon on, music and aromas filled the air continuously. Rich found the atmospheric influences as beneficial, certainly as calming, as anything else he tried over the years. In the end, it was the medical community that learned from Rich. As a part of their field work, interns often spent time at Rich's house. They came, they observed, and they learned.

"The saddest part, the hardest time," Rich said, "during all those years was when my mom went through the physically abusive stage."

It started with her verbally abusive stage, which lasted for years. "My mother was a kind, tender woman," Rich said. "Never said a bad word about anyone, but somewhere along the line, she learned every swear word in the book. And I think she made some up, too."

Once, when Rich and his mother were sitting in the waiting room at the doctor's office, she watched a woman for some time and then said, "My God, that is the fattest woman I have ever seen." After an uncomfortable silence, she finished: "And ugly too. My God, she's ugly."

But the worse was yet to come: the physically abusive stage, the wild and erratic behavior. She would hit, bite, and scratch: combining all three if she had the chance. She grew so uncontrollable at one point that Rich had to hold her still while the doctor injected Haldol in her arm to calm her. Over a two month period, Rich found himself turning to the drug to calm her. "It was the most horrible thing in my life," he said. "Sticking that needle in her arm. Using that drug on her. She was like a noodle after I gave it to her. I could lift an arm and it would drop like dead weight."

But he was desperate during this time and afraid that he might get overly physical in restraining her. He was afraid, he confessed, that he might even hit her. "I only used that drug a few times," he said, pausing. "It was absolutely the worst two months of my life." Fortunately this phase in her decline was a short one.

The next phase, however, was almost as alarming. She turned her physical aggression against herself. She scratched herself until she bled. He cut her nails and put gloves on her, but she persisted, scratching until she'd wear through the gloves. Finally, Rich restrained one arm. It was always the left hand that she used and he found a prescription restraint that allowed some freedom of the hand without allowing her to harm herself. Almost to the end though, she would try to scratch herself during a bath and she succeeded more than once in ripping the skin open.

"What did I learn in my experience? Well, all kinds of medical terms and procedures," he answered, smiling and laughing heartily.

After his laughter subsided, he explained that he learned to be a better person. He learned that you are stronger than you think and you are capable of more than you imagine. He learned there is humor in nearly all situations and that it's not disrespectful to recognize the humor, it's simply acknowledging the human side of the story. He learned patience and tolerance: absolutely essential traits when you are caregiving. But mostly he learned – and this surprised him – that caregiving simply made him feel better. That he felt better in his head than he had in years.

There were simple things that got him through the really rough years of caregiving, like remembering how his parents and his aunt were before they got sick. Not always an easy trick. One of Rich's brothers reached a point where he simply couldn't stand to see their mother anymore. It broke his heart to see his mother so diminished and helpless and, at times, crazy. And he worried that Rich would not remember her the way she used to be.

But there were moments – "little windows," Rich called them – during the caregiving when his mother's eyes looked clear and she'd recognize Rich and smile at him. These little windows lasted almost to the end and during them Rich saw the woman that she had been: the warm eyes, the loving smile, the tender touch. Sometimes, during one of these moments, she'd smile at Rich and say softly, "My baby." Rich was the youngest.

———————

His aunt, who had lived with Rich for ten years, was the first of the three to die. On the morning that she died, after Rich had bathed her and feed her and set her up in her chair by the window, she waved Rich close so she could speak to him.

"You have been good to me," she said, her voice weak but her eyes warm. "Thank you." She died peacefully later that afternoon.

His father, who had had many good days during his decline, became completely unmanageable in the end and spent his last weeks in the hospital. Though it was difficult sending his father away, Rich managed to visit him every day.

And his mother, who had initially declined the fastest, outlived all three of them. When she died, Rich had been caregiving in his home for thirteen consecutive years.

Rich, however, never felt that caregiving was a sacrifice. Even in the last years – when he rose at two a.m. to help each of them to the bathroom and then rose again at six a.m. to feed his mother Ensure, a liquid food supplement, a single sip at a time – Rich knew that his mother, his father, and his aunt were surrounded by family members who loved them and that they never suffered.

On the day his mother died, Rich decided not bring her out to the chair by the window in the sitting room. He fed her, bathed her, and put her in bed for the day. She smiled one last time at Rich as he covered her with a light blanket, and Rich kissed her on the forehead. That last smile, Rich said, meant everything to him.

And, yes, he'd do it all over again.

Dementia

Dementia is NOT a normal part of aging!

Causes of Dementia:

56 % Alzheimer's Disease

14 % Vascular (TIAs, strokes)

12 % Multiple causes (several diseases at once)

 8 % Parkinson's Disease

 6 % other causes

Helpful skills for the caregiver:

+ Approach at eye level in a calm manner, and slightly from the side
+ Simplify: Break tasks down into simple steps for your parent. Give him two or three choices. (In other words, don't ask "What do you want for dinner?" Ask, "Would you like steak or chicken?")
+ Routine: Keep the daily schedule consistent so your parent can anticipate what comes next. Fill routine with appropriate activity: things that won't be over-stimulating.
+ Hand over hand assist: As your parent begins an activity, place your hand on hers. Gently move her hand to do the tasks, until she is comfortable doing it on her own.
+ Evoke positive emotions: avoid arguments and power struggles, focus on things that bring out comfortable and safe feelings
+ Reassure: comfort, reassure, be agreeable, go with the flow of patient
+ Redirect: distract to another activity if your parent is getting agitated or doing something undesirable
+ Re-approach: if what needs to be done is not happening, wait and re-approach at a later time instead of forcing conflict.
+ Choose your battles!

Alzheimer's Disease

What is Alzheimer's Disease (AD)?

Alzheimer's is a type of dementia that effects the brain's comprehension. It is a progressive and terminal disease that can last 2-20 years (average 8 years). There are 2 types: early onset (age 40-60) & late onset (average age of 70). 4 ½ million people have Alzheimer's Disease in the United States. AD is the 4th leading cause of death in older adults. It affects 10% of people over 65, and 50% of those over 85. 1 out of 3 families are affected. Currently, there is no effective reduction or cure for AD, but many advances are on the horizon.

Diagnosis:

Early diagnosis is critical. There are several disorders that can look like Alzheimer's. Before concluding that a person has AD, rule out the following reversible and treatable diagnoses:

Depression, Drug interactions, Thyroid disturbance, Malnourishment, Dehydration, Fluctuating blood sugars, Infections (including Urinary Tract Infection and Pneumonia), Tumor or head trauma

Three Stages of Alzheimer's

Stage 1: WARNING SIGNS, lasting 2-4 years

· Recent memory loss that affects job skills
· Difficulty performing familiar tasks
· Problems with language
· Disorientation of time and place
· Poor or decreased judgment
· Problems with abstract thinking
· Misplacing things
· Change in mood or behavior
· Change in personality
· Loss of initiative

Stage 2: lasting 2-10 years
· Increasing memory loss
· Repetitive statements or movements
· Restless, especially late afternoon or night (Sundowning)
· Suspicious, irritable, agitated
· Fixed ideas that are not real, telling stories that are not true
· Seeing and hearing things that are not there
· Wandering*

Stage 3 : lasting 1-3 years
· Cannot recognize family or self
· Little or no capacity for self care
· Cannot communicate with words
· Cannot control bowel or bladder
· May have seizures, skin breakdown, difficulty swallowing
· Prone to infections

Risk factors for Alzheimer's Disease:
Age
Family History
Female
Low education/occupational level
Hypertension
High cholesterol

* Alzheimer's Association *Safe Return*® is a nationwide identification, support and enrollment program that provides assistance when a person with Alzheimer's or a related dementia wanders and becomes lost locally or far from home.

Assistance is available 24 hours a day, 365 days a year. If an enrollee is missing, one call immediately activates a community support network to help reunite the lost person with his or her caregiver.

www.alz.org/we_can_help_safe_return.asp

A Fairy Tale Ending
Laura's Story

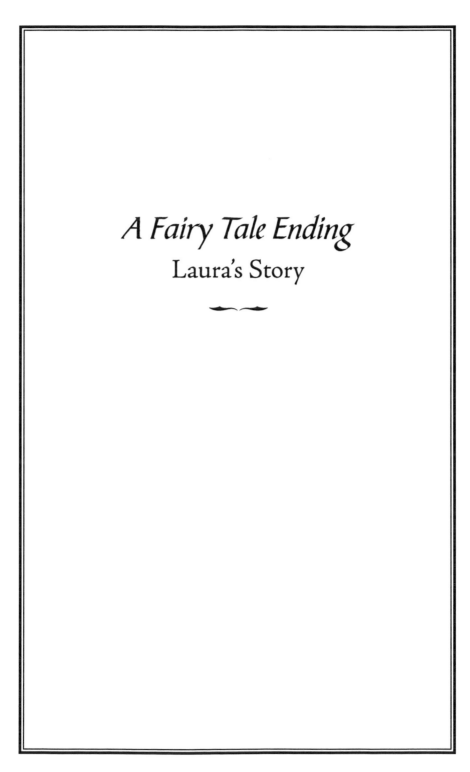

He has a gentle salve for the wounded
A pillow for the weary soul
The only hope for some broken hearts
He is time, and he'll make us whole

We're all healing, healing,
Healing in the hands of time
We're all healing, healing,
Healing in the hands of time

He's taking us all on a journey
He knows exactly every inch of this road
And if we could only see farther down it
We would know…as he knows

It it's much too big today to handle
Just hand it all over to him
Father Time, the master of surprises
Will surprise us once again

We're all healing, healing,
Healing in the hands of time
We're all healing, healing,
Healing in the hands of time

"Healing in the Hands of Time"
by Karen Taylor-Good and Lisa Aschmann

A Fairy Tale Ending

I grew up in Central Arizona, the baby of three kids in a very close knit family. Both my father's and mother's families lived nearby so I spent rough and tumble summers with my aunts, uncles and cousins. I feel like I had a charmed childhood. My mom and dad were wonderful. My mom was a tough and incredibly smart person who had to drop out of high school when she started having kids. I know that always bothered her but she was a very devoted mother and she loved us dearly. When I was little she worked in the cafeteria at my school so she could have the same hours we did. She was always there for us.

My dad was a quiet and gentle man who worked on the railroad his whole life. He had a wonderful deep voice and we loved listening to his stories about life on the rails. I remember my parents being very much in love. When I was young, their relationship seemed magical. My mom always said they were living "happily ever after." And I just took it for granted that they'd always be together. But when my dad turned 58 he started getting disoriented and forgetful. My mom noticed it first of course, since we were all off on our own by then. It turned out to be fast moving Alzheimer's and my dad died when he was only 60. Officially an aneurysm killed him but I really think he died of Alzheimer's. My mom was heartbroken.

But she was a strong and gutsy woman and she turned her pain into something positive. After my dad died she went back to school and became a nurse LPN. She loved to take care of people so becoming a nurse made perfect sense. The ironic thing is that even though she had medical training and cared for others professionally, she didn't take care of herself at all. Maybe it was her generation or just plain stubbornness but she refused to take care of her health. She existed on fried foods and candy. And she smoked like a chimney. She loved cigarettes. Because of this, she ended up having a lot of medical problems. She had a hysterectomy and a tumor in her breast. She had a hernia, blocked carotid arteries and a ton of other things. I counted them up once and I think she had fifteen surgeries, one right after another. Here she was a nurse, who refused to take her own advice about staying healthy.

A few years after my dad died, my mom remarried. She was married to my stepfather for nearly 20 years and I think they were happy. Naturally, when he got sick, she nursed him for the rest of his life. This took an enormous toll on her own health. But even though she was 80 and quite frail when he died, she decided to move out of the house they'd shared and buy herself a huge new house to live in. That was just so her. At age 80 buying a new house. And she wouldn't take anything from my stepfather's estate. She was so proud and independent that she said, "I'm only taking what I brought into the marriage" and she took her furniture and that's all.

She hired someone to come in to cook and clean, and it all seemed to work fine until she was diagnosed with colon cancer. That really was the beginning of the end. The doctors thought they got all the cancer during the surgery but three years later she was in excruciating pain and they couldn't figure out why. She couldn't take care of the house and the woman she'd hired as a companion didn't want to work as many hours as my mom needed. So my mom asked my brother and sister and me to help fill in. The plan was that my brother would go down one weekend, my sister the next and then me. But it never worked out that way. My brother pretty much kept to the schedule but my sister would always have something going and she could never do it. My sister never had time for my mom. She'd lost a daughter to colon cancer and I think she was dealing with her own grief over that. Also, her husband was an alcoholic and I think she was dealing with a lot more than I even knew during that period.

Anyway, the arrangement didn't last long. My mom was in too much pain and needed more care than she was willing to admit. So one weekend I went down and said, "Mom, you can't live like this. You've got to do something. Do you want to come and live with us and we can take care of you?" Now, for a proud, strong woman like my mom to admit that she couldn't be on her own anymore was really difficult. She didn't say anything right away. But after a minute she looked at me and almost in a whisper she said, "Yes."

We packed her up that very day. She was 84 and had been living alone for three years and within 24 hours she was living with us in our house. We cleared all the furniture out of the dining room and put in her bedroom furniture, clothes, TV, and everything else she needed. Luckily, we had a full bath on the first floor for her, so the whole situation worked out well.

My husband was actually the one who suggested she move in with us. He was very understanding. And my mom was careful not to put any stress on us. The biggest issue was her smoking but she agreed to only smoke on the porch. My mom's health was terrible but she just wouldn't give up those cigarettes! And her teeth were rotten because she loved candy and ate it constantly. She rarely ate any real food. Basically she lived on coffee and candy. She'd have an occasional piece of quiche or a bowl of bean soup but that was about it. She was a nurse and she'd only eat food that was loaded with fat and sugar! She weighed about 86 pounds when we she moved in, and when she died two years later, she was even lighter. She didn't put on an ounce of weight during this time, but my husband and I sure did.

Bringing someone into your house is an enormous commitment but the fact is I'm my mother's daughter. I loved my mother dearly and I was so happy to be able to do this for her at the end of her life. And I like to care for needy people just like she did. It really was okay because my mother was ready to hand over the reins of her life to me. I was the one making all the decisions for her and she was fine with that. Dealing with her medications, going to the doctor, making different appointments. I was willing to take it all on and she was willing to have me do it. She was so sweet. One day we were out to lunch and out of the blue she grabbed my hand and said, "We've switched roles haven't we, Laura? You're the mom now and I'm the child." I just squeezed her hand a little tighter and said, "Yeah, mom. And that's sure okay with me." And she said, "That's okay with me too."

But I don't want to sugarcoat the whole thing either. At times, we fought like cats and dogs, and in some ways, she drove me completely nuts. She lied constantly and that really made me crazy. I'd say, "Mom, that's not right" and she would insist it was. She lied her whole life. Ever since I was little she'd told the most outrageous lies. If you asked her why, she'd say, "I don't know. It's just fun." It's like she wanted to live in a fairy tale. One lie she told over and over was that she'd been diagnosed with cancer and was dying. She told this to her dentist, her financial advisor, the woman who did her hair...and it simply wasn't true. Not at that point anyway. I think she wanted to believe she was dying. I think she really wanted to die and just be over with it and out of this world. The truth is she prayed everyday that she wouldn't wake up.

During the time my mom lived with me, my brother and sister were almost no help. We'd already done her estate planning and I was the executor of the will. She'd made it clear that she did not want to be resuscitated if anything like that happened. And we eventually sold or donated everything in her house and she was fine with all that. But the day-to-day responsibility of her care was totally mine and that was draining. My brother did come up every week to see my mom and to give me a break, which helped a lot. And my sister helped when she could. But it was mostly up to me. I tried to keep life for all of us as normal as possible. My mom had her hair done every Thursday. We shopped. We went to church. We took her down to the beach on vacation. She had a dowager's hump and she loved having her back scrubbed so I got a shower seat for her and scrubbed her back when she showered. She said it felt like heaven.

She continued to feel a lot of pain so we took her to a pain specialist who thought the pain stemmed from her osteoporosis. She told him he was wrong. She was certain she had cancer again. She explained it as a tightness around her waist that felt like a rubber band being pulled tighter and tighter, but the doctor didn't agree with her diagnosis. He prescribed a morphine pill for the pain and a variety of other medications. Since she was sleeping well each night and had a tendency to exaggerate, we just sort of let it go and got on with our routine.

Nearly two years after she moved in with us and just before we were getting ready to go to the beach for week, she said something was bothering her on her stomach. On someone else it would have looked like a roll of fat but she didn't have any rolls of fat and I told her we really needed to have a doctor look at it. I figured if it were something serious that required surgery, we could get that done after we returned from the beach.

The doctor ordered an ultrasound and a CAT scan and when my mom came out of the ultrasound she said, "It's something bad. I'm not sure what it is but it looks like it's everywhere in my body." She was home asleep when I drove back to her doctor to get her medications and he just matter-of-factly said, "She's got pancreatic cancer and it's everywhere." I said, "What?" And he said "Your mom's got cancer and it's everywhere."

Of course I started crying and all he said was, "Now, don't fall apart on me." Does that sound like a sensitive thing for a doctor to say? He told me she had two or three months to live and I believed him. Why wouldn't I? I had no way of knowing she'd be dead in two weeks. I walked out of that doctor's office in shock, but the one bit of comfort I had was that she'd be with us for a few more months. That's what he said and I held tight to that. I loved my mom so much I just wasn't ready to let her go.

Telling my mom the news was a lot harder than I thought it would be. I was devastated and I wasn't at all sure how she'd react. I took her out to lunch the next day and on the way home I said, "Mom, I've got something to tell you. You've got cancer and the doctor says you've only got about two to three months to live." And you know what she said? "Laura, you have just made me the happiest person in the world. Now I can finally see your dad again." She said she couldn't remember what her second husband looked like, "but I know every inch of your dad's face like it was my own."

Looking back, I wish I would have pushed harder with her first doctor after she had the surgery for the colon cancer. And again with the pain specialist. Maybe if we'd caught the cancer earlier…well…you just don't know. I thought the doctors knew what they were talking about and I let them do what they thought was right, but you can't do that. I should have insisted they order another MRI and another CAT scan. You have to be proactive. But in the end my mom got what she wanted. She wanted to see my dad and live in their fairy tale again.

Hospice came in the very next day and said the morphine she'd been taking hadn't been working because of her colon problems and she couldn't absorb the pills. She needed liquid morphine instead. So she really had been in terrible pain. That hadn't been a lie. We considered canceling our trip to the beach but my mom insisted we stick with our plans. She hadn't wanted to go anyway and would be staying with my sister. Of course we were thinking she had several months left to live so we agreed to leave. Before we left we conferred with hospice about what to do, we got her settled at my sister's, and we called all her friends to let them know she only had a few months to live. They all called and talked to her and made plans to come and see her.

We had a terrific week at the beach under the mindset that when we got back we were going to have a couple of hard months ahead with my mom. While we were gone my mom had a great time at my sister's mostly because she loved sitting out next to my sister's pond smoking those damn cigarettes! And hospice had finally gotten her pain under control with the liquid morphine. She came back to our house feeling a lot more comfortable.

Unfortunately, the week following our vacation turned into a nightmare. My daughter Donna ended up in the hospital again after a serious surgery. She'd had surgery and had given birth to my grandchild, Anna, only a couple months before. Suddenly I felt pulled in fifteen different directions. Donna needed me, my new grandchild needed me, and my mother was dying. It felt like I was being torn apart. That's the downside of being there for everyone. It's incredibly stressful and exhausting. Plus I had church activities and community commitments. I had way too much going on!

I spent a lot of time at the hospital that weekend and luckily by Tuesday evening, Donna was well enough to go home. I called my husband to tell him the news and in the background I heard my mom yell out, "Tell her to stop and get me some onion chips from White Castle." I tell you she just loved junk food. When I got home, my mom ate the chips, and on the way back to her bedroom, she grabbed my face and kissed me and said, "Thank-you, darling." At the time, I thought she was thanking me for the chips but looking back, I think she was saying thank-you for a whole lot more.

The next morning she slipped into a coma. The hospice nurse came and said her blood pressure was very low. She told me my mother was dying but I was thinking, "that's impossible." She has another couple of months to live. And only last night she was eating onion chips from White Castle! My sister came over and we spent the day in my mom's room. When my sister left, I lay down next to my mom in her bed. I was talking to her about this and that. I'm not even sure she heard me but I just wanted to be near her. She was bent over and lying in a fetal position on her left side. Her body was so little. It really did almost feel like she was my child. I was facing her, lying there thinking, "Mom don't die. You're not supposed to die yet." I was scared. After a little while, my husband came in and said, "You've got to let her go." I knew he was right. He left us alone and after a few minutes I whispered to her, "Mom, it's OK. You can go. I'm going to be just fine."

And then she died, just like that. She started foaming at the mouth, which I didn't know was a common thing that happens right before death, and then she was gone. The thing is, I thought she had three months left to live. I was still thinking about her living, not dying. Four days earlier she'd been out on the deck, holding court with all her grandkids and smoking her cigarettes. On Wednesday our minister had come and given her communion and by Thursday she was dead.

Looking back, I can say that one thing I did right was involving my church right from the time my mom started living with us. People donated food and stopped by and really supported us the whole time. I asked for help early on and I got it. If you don't ask, nobody will know you need the help. And even with the help, I still had way too much going on in my life during this period. If you commit to taking care of a parent, especially in your own home, you have to start saying no to other things. You have to prioritize and not take on more than you have to or you'll burn out and that's not helpful to anyone. This experience also taught me how important it is to use the time you are given on this earth well. Only do what you feel passionate about on any particular day because it might truly be your last.

Even though I know that I did everything possible for my mom, I still feel she was taken from me just a little too fast. I keep fixating on the fact that she'd eaten those damn onion chips only hours before she died. My husband always says, "Your mom probably had so much gas from all that junk food that she just flew to heaven." And I know he's trying to make me feel better. The fact is my mother was one tough cookie. She was in control of everything in her life right up to the very end. She was the one who decided she was going to die on her own timetable, not the timetable the doctor had given her and she was ready. She did it in her own time. And in her own way. And now she and my father are together again, living happily ever after, just like she always wanted.

Legal Documents

...are written, signed, dated, and notarized documents that transfer authority as needed. All documents need to be completed while the principal (the person who the documents affect) is still competent and should be done now for your aging parent, you, and any of your adult children. Keep the originals at home or in a safe-deposit box and give copies to your doctor, relatives, banks, and attorneys.

Wills

Creating a *will* can be the beginning for an estate plan. Through a will, you transfer assets titled in your sole name to beneficiaries. It is a way to let your beneficiaries, including loved ones and charities, know your wishes for the distribution of your estate. You name an executor in your will who oversees the settlement of your estate after your death and works with an attorney to comply with any probate reporting requirements. Probate is a legal process used with wills to settle an estate. Unfortunately, information about the value of your assets, your outstanding liabilities and distribution of your estate must be filed on public record.

A *will* allows for an orderly distribution of assets. If the principal (person whose will it is) does not write a will to say how he wants his estate divided, then the estate is divided according to state law. Contact your local Bar Association for assistance or to locate a lawyer. Now is a good time to make sure your parent has a will and you do too!

Financial Durable Power of Attorney

Financial Durable Power of Attorney allows the aging parent (principal) to authorize another person (agent) to manage his affairs in case of incapacity. It can be revoked by the principal. The agent acts in the best interest of the principal. It is only in effect during the principal's lifetime. It is also a good idea to add a trustee or relative to principal's checking account.

Trusts

Certain types of *trusts* can shelter assets from estate taxes and give you greater control over their management and distribution. Unlike a will, use of a trust is a private way to transfer assets to beneficiaries. With a *living trust*, your estate can avoid probate. You can name a trustee to manage your estate during your lifetime should you become unable to act on your behalf and prevents the need for guardianship. You can be a beneficiary of the trust while living and name other beneficiaries to receive your assets after you die. If you provide for continuation of your trust after your death, the assets you provided for your loved ones can be protected from creditors, lawsuits and divorce.

All assets (including car, house, bank accounts) should be transferred by re-titling them to the trust. Very high-valued assets can be placed in different trusts.

Medical Documents

...also known as Advanced Directives, allow the patient (principal) to let physicians and others know his wishes for medical care if the principal is not coherent enough to tell them. The patient needs both a living will and durable power of attorney for healthcare. It is strongly suggested that everyone have these as soon as they turn 21. Up to 50% of people cannot make their own decisions at end-of-life. Each state has different regulations. Please check with your doctor's office, hospital social services, or on-line.

Durable Power of Attorney for Health Care

Durable Power of Attorney for Health Care is similar to the Financial Durable Power of Attorney, but for health care decisions. It allows the aging parent (principal) to authorize another person (agent) to manage her health care decisions when a physician makes the determination that the principal cannot make decisions regarding her own health. This agent can make sure her physicians carry out her wishes for medical treatment should she become unable to make and communicate her decisions.

This document is needed in conjunction with a Living Will, because it covers medical treatments and situations that Living Wills do not cover, including health decisions that are not related to terminal illness. It is highly recommended that everyone have a Durable Power of Attorney for Health Care.

Living Will

A *Living Will* is a document that expresses the parent's (principal's) wishes for medical treatment in the case where she becomes incapacitated. The Living Will needs to be created while the principal is still competent. It describes the principal's wishes in terms of life-support, extraordinary medical treatment, and care which artificially or technologically postpones death. The Living Will supersedes a durable power of attorney for health care with respect to life sustaining care decisions. An oral request by the principal to a physician, family member, or health care worker revokes the signed agreement. It is highly recommended that everyone have a Living Will because it takes the burden off of the family and makes decisions easier for everyone. A Living Will can also allow for a natural death process, if that is what the principal wishes.

Do Not Resuscitate (DNR)

Do Not Resuscitate (DNR) orders can be a part of a living will. DNR states that no heroic or extraordinary measures should be taken in the case of terminal illness. If the principal is dying, the physicians are not supposed to interfere.

HIPAA release form

Due to the Health Insurance Portability and Accountability Act of 1996 (HIPAA), doctors cannot talk to other people about their patients or patients' health. To allow adult children or caretakers access to health information and to talk to the doctors, a *HIPAA release form* should be filled out. Ask each doctor or hospital for one.

Location of Documents

Keep the originals at home or in a safe-deposit box and give copies to your doctor, relatives, banks, and attorneys.

Documents that should be copied and given to others:
Will
Durable Power of Attorneys
Trusts
Living Will
Medicare card
Insurance cards
Social Security card
Car titles, real estate deeds, appraisals
Birth and Marriage certificates

Either give relatives the following or alert them as to where you keep this information:

Full name

Date of Birth

Caregiver names

Family names, addresses, phone numbers

Friends' names, addresses, phone numbers

Clergy, Doctor, Lawyer, Accountant, Insurance Agent, etc. names

Bank name and account numbers

Insurance policies

Investments, investment firms, account numbers

List of medications

Location of safe deposit box and keys

Last 3 years tax filings

Retirement plans (IRA, 401k, military benefits, pensions, etc.)

Hindsight is 20-20
Jan's Story

Sometimes love means holding on with all your heart and soul
But now I've learned at last I know
Sometimes love means letting go

Now my Daddy is ready to leave this earth
And move on to what comes next
And I'm hanging on to him for all I'm worth
When a voice inside me softly says

Sometimes love means holding on with all your heart and soul
But now I've learned at last I know
Sometimes love means letting go

"Sometimes Love Means Letting Go"
By Karen Taylor-Good and Jason Blume

Hindsight is 20-20

My father lived nearly a thousand miles away when he became depressed and lost forty pounds in two months. He wandered into his doctor's office – gaunt, confused, and dirty – asking for food and help. They thought he was a homeless man. It breaks my heart to think of it, but it is only in hindsight that I recognized all the warning signs of his rapid decline.

My father was always active and strong. A hunter. A fisherman. A traveler. Mr. Fix-It. "He did it all and then some," my sister Judy always says. He lived life with gusto and had an infectious smile. When he smiled, everyone in the room smiled. More importantly, he was a kind and loving parent. He was always the rock of strength in my life. Even long distance, he was always there for me.

I think that's why I missed so many signs of his decline. Or, perhaps, that's why I refused to accept so many warning signs of his decline. A parent is the one who nurtures you; a parent is the one that you always depend on. Even after they are gone.

After my mother died 17 years ago, my father remarried and moved from Indiana to Texas. We spoke often on the phone during these years, and I saw him a few times every year. He always spent the holidays with my family or with Judy's family, thus remaining very much in our lives even though so many miles separated us.

My father had a very active social life in his last years. After his second wife died, he had a lady friend, who subsequently died. With yet another lady friend, he moved onward, and our lives so far away moved forward also. A life with me as a caregiver never crossed my mind.

Then he began to slow down. He and his lady friend, Mildred, began playing cards at her home rather than going dancing or to the movies. And then my father's heart gave him trouble and he had heart surgery. He subsequently spent four months recovering with Judy in Indiana.

After four months though, my father insisted on returning to Texas. "One more winter," he rationalized. Though somewhat physically diminished, he still seemed vital and capable of caring for himself. More importantly, Judy and I struggled with an issue that numerous children will face as their parents age: Do you do what intuitively feels right? Or do you honor your parent's wishes?

We chose to honor his wishes. On more winter in Texas didn't seem out of his control. Little did we know.

In retrospect, we can see that his decline began almost immediately. I remember him being confused on the phone occasionally, but when I'd call later or the next day to check on him, he was fine. I know now, though, that our socially-active father became very withdrawn and depressed.

We suspect that he gave up during this time. His lady friend, Mildred, had passed away while he was recovering from heart surgery, so he never even had a chance to grieve with her family. More of his friends died and he stopped going to Friends Club, the social club for seniors which had always provided him with companionship and social activity. And my father's cat, an ever-present companion, also died during this time. I believe it was simply too much. The deaths along with his diminished physical capabilities overwhelmed him and he withdrew from the world completely.

I remember my surprise when he told me on the phone that he didn't know if he should be driving very far anymore and that he was hungry. I didn't connect "hungry" and "not driving very far" to "I'm not going to the grocery store for food and I need help." Hindsight is indeed 20-20. And I know now that we should have acted right then. Remember, this is the man who cooked huge gourmet dinners for himself and had a refrigerator full of vegetables from his own garden. Or so I thought.

When my father actually asked for help, we thought surely he could wait until summer. A few months, no more. Judy is a teacher; she couldn't get away at a moment's notice. My husband and I were selling our house in Maryland and moving back to North Carolina, not to mention preparing for my daughter's high school graduation. But, as I've learned, the active pace of your life doesn't slow down when a parent needs help, it simply speeds up.

When the doctor called to tell me that our father had wandered into his office confused and starving, I couldn't believe it. How did our father slip so quickly? How did we miss it? Our lives were still busy, but we had to act and the doctor, bless him, helped us get Dad set up with meals delivered to his house every day. His neighbors promised to check in on him, too. "All he needs to do is ask," a neighbor said, "if he needs a ride to the grocery store or to the doctor. Anything." But my Dad never asked for anything in his life. He never wanted to be a burden to anyone.

The days dragged. I spoke with my father every day. Summer finally came. My daughter graduated, my husband and I sold our house and moved to North Carolina. Judy and I went to Texas, sold my father's house, tied up all his loose ends, and moved him to assisted living in North Carolina. I was not working at the time, so Judy and I decided to move him to North Carolina because I would have more time to spend with him than she would.

And I'm glad that I had those last months near him. He had become a shell of the man that I knew and loved. He had a multitude of health problems and was emotionally less mature than a three-year-old. My father announced very casually one day that he needed to relieve himself and proceeded to do so in front of me; I saw nurses lift him by his ankles like a baby and change his diapers. At that time, it became very clear to me that my family and I were faced with the toughest questions and choices that a caregiver can face: Are we helping him get better? Or are we simply prolonging a dignified death?

For all practical matters, my father was already gone. He had become despondent and had a multitude of health problems. "I'm amazed his heart is strong enough to keep pumping at all," his doctor told me. I prayed now for his life to be pain-free and his end to be peaceful rather than praying for any sort of recovery. And one afternoon when Judy and I spoke, I finally worked up the courage to tell her how fast he was declining and that I thought it was time to let him go if anything happened. I told her I thought that's what he would want. Judy, who wasn't witnessing his daily decline, disagreed. She still envisioned the man that she saw two months prior and believed that any measure possible to keep him alive should be taken. I wanted to scream that I'm the one seeing him every day; I'm the one at his bedside. I wanted to scream, "He doesn't even know me!" But I didn't.

Judy came to visit shortly after that phone call and she saw first-hand how quickly his health and mind had deteriorated. We had also scheduled a lunch with our friend Barbara who wanted to interview us for a book she was writing a book on caregiving. I knew it was an opportunity for me to approach a difficult subject.

We told Barbara the whole story: his heart attack, the signs of deterioration that we missed when our father was in Texas, the depression, his withdrawal from the world and sudden collapse. And we spoke of happy memories, of when we were kids and went ice fishing with our father. He would shovel off a big patch of ice for us before he fished, so we could be with him. It's a treasured memory, skating with my sister on a cold winter morning, our skates scraping across rough ice, our breath shooting out in funnels, the sun bright, the sky blue, our laughter, and my father watching us and smiling. Always smiling.

When Barbara asked how he was getting along in assisted living, Judy nearly broke down. His rapid decline had completely taken her by surprise. It's one thing to know that a parent is weakening and becoming despondent, and completely another to see it, to feel it viscerally, to have your father look you in the eyes and turn away as though he had no idea who you were. Judy told me later that she felt like someone punched her in the stomach when she first saw him.

Every word I spoke that afternoon I addressed to Barbara, but it was really for my sister. I looked into Barbara's eyes, but I emptied my soul to my sister. "I am ready to let my father go," I said. "I think that is the caring and heartfelt approach to take now. I think that is what he would want."

Judy sat silently. Even after seeing him that morning, she still wasn't ready to address the issue. I told Barbara that my husband believed if the doctors could simply diagnose my father's health problems correctly than he could be restored to the man he had been. That my husband believed modern medicine would triumph. I believe that my husband was simply not ready to let go. Besides, I told Barbara (and my sister) even if they discover exactly what is wrong, my father is not strong enough for surgery. Let alone multiple surgeries to address all his problems.

"You always want to hang on as long as you can," I said, "because you have that hope that he might get back to the way he was. But he's not." There was a silence between us and then Judy, her voice filled with emotion, said, "No, he's not." It was the first time she had said it and she stopped talking so she could control her emotions and then finished: "I don't want him to suffer. I don't want him to be a vegetable. I want him back like he was and he can't be."

At that point Judy went for tissue and came back, crying and laughing softly, with the whole box. "I think we'll need these," she said.

Her comment broke the tension, and then it happened: the phone rang. I walked to another room to answer it, and a nurse told me that our father was experiencing full-blown cardiac arrest. "What do you want us to do?" he asked.

I exhaled, cradled the phone in two hands on my chest and walked back to Judy and Barbara. I exhaled again and stood there with the phone on my chest. "What?" Judy asked. And I heard myself saying, "Dad's in full-blown cardiac arrest."

There was a moment of complete unbelievable, frozen silence; I remember hearing a clock tick in another room. I was completely stunned and empty after our emotional and tearful lunch. Judy spoke and the world moved again. "Then let him go," she said. And, choking back emotion, she managed to ask, "Can they keep him comfortable?"

I told the nurse to let him go; Judy and I sat at the table stunned. Barbara offered to drive us to the hospital, but we needed to just sit for a time. I felt the emotion welling up in my body; my father was dying at that very moment. My father – the rock in my life – was slipping from this world. "He waited for me to come home," Judy said. "He waited for me, I know it."

"Yes," I answered, "He waited for you to come home. I know it too."

Elder Depression

Although depression is common in older Americans, it is not a normal part of aging.

Sadness and grief are normal and resolve over time. The person is still able to feel joy in the midst of their mourning. Depression lasts longer, rarely goes away on its own, and does not allow for joy.

Symptoms:

Poor health, change in amount of sleep, anxious, loss of interest or passion, loss of energy, decreased concentration, loss of worthiness, sad mood, irritability, confusion, weight changes, negative thinking, withdrawal, persistent moodiness, vague health complaints, social withdrawal, irritable/demanding behavior, lack of attention to personal care, confusion, hopelessness, suicidal thoughts

Treatment:

Depression can often go undiagnosed, because it is not recognized by family and doctors. Depression can look like other illness or dementia. A way to differentiate between dementia and depression is to look at the speed (dementia is gradual, depression is rapid) and the memory loss (dementia has memory loss, depression doesn't). Depression is real. Treatment works. Get medical help. When getting medical help, remember that treatment with medicine may take trying different drugs and then different dosage changes to get it just right. Stick with it, and change doctors if you need to. It may take 4-6 weeks for medicine to take affect.

Many elderly do NOT get treatment because they think that depression is just a part of growing old, that it is a character flaw or weakness, or that treatment is too expensive.

Most elderly who commit suicide, have seen a doctor in the last several months.

Causes:

Isolation, major life change or loss, hereditary tendency, alcohol or drug addiction, previous history of depression, difficulty adjusting to stress and change, side effects of other medicines, concurrent illnesses (Parkinson's, Alzheimer's, Cancer, Diabetes, stroke), vascular changes in the brain, injuries, head traumas, poor health

Statistics:

Depression affects 15-20% of people over 65 years of age (6.5 million). Only 1 out of 6 is treated appropriately. Women are twice as likely to be diagnosed with depression. A suicide attempt is a desperate call for help. Men are 6 times more likely to commit suicide. The rate of suicide is highest in those over 75 years of age.

Ask a Question – Save a Life:

Asking the question will not cause someone to commit suicide. It is not being intrusive if you are trying to save a person's life. Persuade the person to talk and seek professional help.

If you ask the elderly if they are depressed, they will most likely answer NO. The following questions are a better way to assess depression.

Questions:
What are you eating?
Are you having any fun?
How are you sleeping?
Do you feel that your family/friends would be better off without you?

The Invisible Club
Caroline's Story

What if everything that makes us sad
Turns out to be not so bad
And everything that seemed so wrong
Was what I needed all along
What if we don't have a clue
What if we're just not meant to
What if everything in life's a gift...What if?

Life's a question a tale untold
We find all the answers as it unfolds
I have learned through trial and tears
That faith is my freedom and it's stronger than fear
And what I've been afraid of
Maybe that's the stuff dreams are made of

What if things that made me cry
Made me stronger by and by
And everything they threw my way
Made me who I am today
What if I'm just finding out
That trust is what it's all about
What if everything in life's a gift...What if?

"What If?"
By Karen Taylor-Good
and Jason Blume and Greg Barnhill

The Invisible Club

My mother was an amazing person. She was ambitious, talented, intelligent and interested in absolutely everything. Art. Philosophy. Music. Everything. And she definitely marched to her own drummer. Everything she did was on her own terms. She was the most strong-willed person I've ever met and when she got sick, I honestly thought she wouldn't die because she didn't want to. I really thought she could keep death from happening because she was so strong. It was almost a shock when death proved stronger.

My relationship with my mother was complicated. When I was growing up our family went through a lot of tough times. I'm the oldest of four children and the only girl. When I was 12 and my youngest brother was five, my mother walked out on us. She just got up and left. She was an alcoholic for 15 years and it tore my family apart. Even before she left she was barely there. She was either disengaged or out on a drinking binge somewhere. You just never knew what was going to happen when she drank. I can remember when I was ten, I was in the play *The Music Man*. I had a solo and I was jumping out of my skin I was so excited. My mother came drunk to every single performance. This was before air conditioning and every night I had to stand up there on stage smelling the alcohol rolling off her. I cried every night of that play.

My parents divorced in the late 1960's in a small town in the Midwest. Nowadays divorce is nothing, but back then it caused such a scandal they actually published a story about it on the front page of the newspaper. Can you imagine? I remember going to school that day and nobody, absolutely nobody would talk to me. Not even my friends. Nobody knew what to say. Back then, nobody got divorced and nobody talked about suburban women alcoholics. You just suffered in silence and so did your family. Instead of treating her alcoholism she was put under psychiatric care. My whole childhood she was in and out of mental hospitals. They were treating her for depression and she probably was depressed, but they never addressed her alcoholism. It was considered a man's problem back then. Down and out drifters were alcoholics, not college-educated suburban women with four young children.

When my mom walked out, my father, bless his soul, held our family together somehow. He was mom, dad, housekeeper and breadwinner all rolled into one. He was like Humpty Dumpty putting our family back together again. He was our salvation but the pressure on him was terrible. He was always in a bad mood, angry and yelling and I was afraid of him. As the oldest and the only girl, I took on a lot of responsibility at a very young age. I was like a mini-mom. I cooked, I did the laundry, and I looked after my younger brothers. When I look at pictures of me from that time, I look 20 years older than I was.

We had dinner at my mom's apartment once a week. My dad would sit outside in the freezing car while we all trooped into her apartment bundled up in our winter coats. It was my job to decide if she was too drunk to see us. If she were, I'd have to bundle everybody up again and march them back out to the car. If she were sober, I'd signal my dad through the window and he would drive away and pick us up later. I dreaded those nights.

When I was in high school my mom moved to another city to attend graduate school. She was a binge drinker so she could operate fine in the world until she went on a binge and then, watch out. When she left town, we pretty much stopped communicating. I missed her terribly but it was actually a relief to have her gone. I feel badly saying it but when she was there, life was too crazy. Like when I was 18 and about to have surgery for a benign tumor. There I was, about to go into the operating room, when my mother showed up so drunk she could barely stand up. A nurse actually had to kick her out of my room.

Her drinking made me so sad. My whole childhood, all I ever wanted was a mom. I had this fantasy about the perfect mom or really any mom at all. My brothers and I glommed onto all our friends' moms. We wanted a mother more than anything. We'd be in the kitchen talking to somebody's mom and our friends would be like "OK, let's go." And we'd be like, "We can't leave now. We're talking to your *mom.*"

But finally, when I was a sophomore in college, my mom got sober. And she was sober from that point on. She was sober for 23 years before she died. I spent a long time being angry at my mom but when she got sober, I forgave her. Becoming a parent myself really helped me forgive my own parents. When I saw how tough the job was, I had a whole new perspective. And I don't think you can overstate the power of forgiveness. No matter how unforgivable the things your parents did to you, if you can find a way to forgive them, it's like a gift you give yourself. So many wonderful things have happened in my life. Why would I want to hang on to the bad stuff when so much good stuff is there too? I'm just not a person who can live being angry or hating someone. That doesn't work for me. Nobody signs up for all the pain you get in life but you have to deal with it and hope that it makes you a more compassionate person. That's what I think, at least.

It's not that I wasn't mad at my mother. Of course I was. But sick people don't make well decisions. And my mother was very sick during much of her life. Anyway, I think my mother suffered a lot more than we did. She wasn't there and she missed our lives growing up while my brothers and I got to grow up together. We saw each other's ballgames and plays and report cards. We were there for each other and my mother missed all that. We didn't suffer nearly as much as she did.

After my mother got sober she worked really hard to create good relationships with my brothers and me. She was very involved in our careers and our lives. She adored her grandchildren and was a wonderful grandma. We spoke to each other often by phone. She was generous and supportive and she did her best. We established a good adult relationship. It wasn't a traditional mother/daughter relationship, but it was a loving relationship. I suppose I was looking for an apology from her but she wasn't one to come out and say, "I'm sorry for this or for that." I think she was too ashamed to talk about it. But she did apologize through her actions. You can't fix things and you can't go back. You can only go forward and try to make amends.

Her whole life my mother was very independent and moved around a lot. She really did her own thing which is probably why it took us all so long to figure out that she was physically ill. She was living on the East Coast at the time and she didn't tell anyone she wasn't feeling well. For some reason my mother didn't have faith in doctors and it's too bad because she died from colon cancer, which is a very preventable cancer. My mother was diagnosed with cancer when she was 68 and she lived only 14 months after the diagnosis. I can tell you right now that colon cancer is not a pleasant way to die. She died in her home, which is how she wanted it. But I think she was ill for some time before she finally went to a doctor. She only went because she was finally on Medicare and in so much pain that she couldn't sit down. My mother didn't have health insurance and money was always an issue for her. Before we knew how sick she really was, she was being treated by a Chinese herbalist. Maybe if she'd had more traditional treatments early on, we might have caught the cancer earlier, but she didn't like doctors. You can't take care of someone who won't go see a doctor.

When we eventually found out how sick my mother was, my brothers and I were all very involved in her care. Looking back I'm not even sure how we did it. Each of us was balancing careers, children, everything. Luckily we had supportive spouses and friends to pitch in. Without them, it would have been impossible. My mom told us she wanted to move back to the Midwest into her grandparents' old farmhouse where she spent summers as a girl. I think she already knew how sick she was but she didn't let on. We just thought it would be wonderful to have her living nearby so with the help of our spouses, we bought the house for her and rehabbed it to make it comfortable.

My youngest brother ended up living with her. His life was sort of a mess at that point and he needed a place to stay. When my mom started to get very sick, my siblings and I actually paid our youngest brother to care for her because she needed someone there and he didn't have a job. In some ways the whole thing was hardest on him because he was actually living there and couldn't get away that often. The rest of us came and stayed for days or weeks at a time depending on our schedules.

Overall, I think we did pretty well. There's a lot of chaos in taking care of someone who is dying, but I think as a family we really pulled together. I took the lead in making decisions about her care and my brothers were fine with that. I think they were relieved that I was willing to take it on. We each took on a different role in her care. One of my brothers developed a close relationship with her internist and he was in charge of asking questions. The other showed up to help whenever he could and my youngest brother was there 24 hours a day. We argued very little about what to do, which I suppose is a little unusual.

Without our supportive families I'm not sure we could have pulled this off. My husband completely took over the care of our two boys so I could be with my mom. My brothers' families did the same. My husband was like "You need to be there and we will manage." I feel so lucky that I had this time with my mom. I don't think my husband got much sleep during this time. And my boys didn't like me being gone but they knew how sick Grandma was. They were just great about it.

I remember a time near the end of her life when I was driving my youngest son to camp and we got the call that Grandma wasn't doing well. We were literally in the car driving out of town and my son, who was nine at the time, said "Mom, I can go to camp anytime. Let's go to Grandma's right now. It'll be like Camp Grandma." And it was. We did our best to keep everything fun and upbeat. My brother took my son fishing while we were there. They played computer games and cards. That's the way my mother wanted it. She didn't want us to just sit around. She enjoyed watching all the activity, watching her son and grandson play ball together outside. Keeping things normal made it more fun for everybody. She was very ill at this time but she did her best to keep life going on around her.

One of the hardest lessons I learned is that when someone is terminally ill, you really have no control over the whole process of dying. That "one day at a time" thing is so annoying, enraging and difficult because it isn't one day at a time. It's one hour at a time. Or one ten-minute walk at a time. You wake up and think the day is going to go one way and instead you end up in the emergency room. Or there's a fever or some other crisis to deal with. You try to plan but everyday is a complete unknown. Control is an illusion, especially when the person is so ill and fragile. I guess I learned that you can't have any expectations.

My mother didn't want to be in the hospital when she died. She was comfortable in her own bed so I'm grateful she was able to die at home. She was in and out of the hospital several times during her illness. She had surgery and chemo and thankfully she did have some good weeks and days. But ultimately she couldn't eat and she was in a lot of pain. Whenever she ended up back at the hospital she worked real hard to get back home. I'm glad we were able to keep her in her home but in some ways, the only time we got a break was when she was in the hospital.

I took on a lot. We all did. But we did it out of love. We had some hospice help with the medical equipment. She was on Medicare so we transferred her medical care to hospice. They were great but we didn't have any nurses. It was me, my brothers and our aunt. Going it alone like that with her at home was hard, especially when I had to be "the bad guy." At one point, my mother was crying constantly and in a lot of pain because she was hungry but couldn't keep anything down. I insisted that Medicare pay for a special food medicine in an IV that was very expensive. I met a lot of resistance because Medicare didn't want to pay for it. But it made my mother much more comfortable and I just knew it was the right thing to do.

To make it happen I had to circumvent the nurse and call my mom's oncologist directly. I did it nicely and politely but firmly. It's not that I didn't know she was dying. I wasn't in denial. I just wanted her to be comfortable. At moments like that I felt very lonely. Those were hard battles but I knew the buck stopped with me. My aunt would look at me. My brothers would look at me and I'd want to scream "I'm not a doctor! I don't know what I'm doing!" But I had to make those kinds of decisions. And I did.

I do regret that I was never brave enough to ask my mother certain things. I wanted to ask her things like was she scared? Was she comfortable dying? Did she feel like God would be there? But I couldn't. We skirted around it. I wish we could have had those conversations. I overheard her talking with other people so I knew some of how she felt but it's hard to know how to bring those things up. You want to be loving and not inflict pain. I didn't want her to feel like I was judging her.

One thing I learned is you should do whatever it takes to get to the side of someone who is dying. Not necessarily to talk or settle things between you but just to be there at the end. Being with a loved one before they die is a priceless memory no one can take away. It's so important. It's not about what's said. You can talk about the weather or what's in the fruit bowl on the table. It's more about being there. People hesitate. They don't want to intrude or they're not sure if they'll be welcome. My advice is to err on the side of going. You won't regret it.

Not long before my mom died my father came up to visit. It was a long trek for him and she'd been ill for a long time already. They'd had such a difficult life together. But he made the trip and they had a wonderful conversation. Like two old friends reminiscing. They had nothing left to fight about and my dad let her take the lead and I think they made their peace with each other. She weighed all of 80 pounds at this point. We have a picture of them together, smiling, and they both look so happy. She died two weeks later.

Caregiving is truly a life-altering and transformational experience. No matter what kind of relationship you have with your parents while they're alive, when a parent is dying you become part of an invisible club that nobody wants to join. People who haven't lost a parent won't understand your loneliness or how busy you are with each new daily crisis. But people who have been through it know what membership in the club means. I can honestly say that despite the tough times with my mom, seeing her go through a terminal illness, caring for her and being there with her when she died was really an incredible gift. It sounds strange. But all my brothers and I ever wanted was a mom. Someone to hold our hands, and take care of us and wipe away our tears. Isn't it funny that at the end of my mother's life *we* were the ones holding *her* hand and taking care of *her*? When she left us that first time so long ago when we were kids, all I felt was pain. But when she left us this time, I truly felt at peace. All I ever wanted was a mom. And now, even though she's gone, I truly feel I had one.

Can we talk?

How to talk so they can listen...

Listen: give the elderly time to speak

No distractions: quiet, comfortable setting

Time: the correct time and enough time

Set the tone: calm and gentle

Don't take anything personally

Pick your battles: do not argue

Redirect: divert when things start to stray or get heated

Watch everyone's body language: it is 55% of all communication

Take it slow: it could be a series of conversations

Share feelings: respond more to feeling than content

Share other people's stories: often they can hear someone else's dilemma

Help: "I want to help you remain in control as long as possible."

Third party: invite a family counselor or mutual professional

Offer questions: not ultimatums

Talk about the past: it is their source of strength

Follow their lead

Visiting – how to fill the silence...

Read/write/make letters and cards

Read out loud short stories, newspaper, Bible

Look at photos and reminisce

Bird watching or even people watching

Talk a walk

Share stories

Brush hair or paint nails

Have a party: celebrate anything/anyone

Bring a pet or child

Play a simple game, a child-like game: Uno, board games

Listen to vintage music

Dance, exercise, or bat around helium balloons
Stroke on lotions and massage
Share how much your relative means to you
Do activities appropriate to the child within them

Talking about concerns...

Do not make the person feel helpless: involve them in the decisions
Research: investigate possible solutions, local Area on Aging
Determine functioning level: acts of daily living, executive functioning
Use "I" statements: keeps them from feeling attacked
State your concerns
State consequences and potential problems
Suggest one change at a time
Suggest a trial period
Validate their feelings

When they refuse help...

Are they concerned with cost?
Do they not see the problem?
Are they concerned with having a stranger in the house?
Do they feel that family should be taking care of chores and/or t hem?
Is making decisions too difficult?

How to talk about financial affairs...

Talking about money is difficult because it is not an acceptable topic if you are elderly and grew up in the Great Depression. When you get intimidated approaching this topic, consider the alternative to never having the talk about medical/financial wishes. In other words, it needs to be done. You can start the conversation with, "I am starting to put together my financial plan... what does yours look like?" or tell them about a friend's financial story or share a story from *Stuck in the Middle*. Sometimes elderly people can hear someone else's problem more easily than their own. Assure them that you only want to help and honor their wishes.

Note: All documents need updating. They should be updated every 3-5 years, if moved to a new state, if there are changes within the family, or if there are changes in the tax code.

Falling Away from the World
Karen's Story

This is the woman who had all the answers
The one I would lean on for comfort, for strength
She's never forgotten one grandchild's birthday
Now she can't remember my name
And it makes me so angry, I shake my fist
And cry out to the heavenly one
Why would you play such a cold-hearted trick?
I thought your job was to love
And the answer came down from above:

She's gonna fly
When her time here is through
First she'll have to let go
Of some things she can't use
'Cause people and places, memories and faces
Are just way too heavy, it seems
To carry on angel's wings.

This is the woman who saw things so clearly
The one who could pick out one crumb on the floor
She saw through a white lie, saw me through love's eyes
She hardly can see anymore.
And it makes me so sad, and it just isn't fair
Why should so much be taken away?
But when I cry out for all that she's lost
I silently hear someone say

She's gonna fly
When her time here is through
First she'll have to let go
Of some things she can't use.

"On Angel's Wings"
by Karen Taylor-Good and Jason Blume

Falling Away from the World

You know that Beatles song *The Long and Winding Road?* That's how it's been with my parents at the end of their lives. I feel like we've been traveling together along a difficult and unfamiliar path slowly finding our way to where we stand today.

Our journey actually began about fifteen years ago. My mom and dad were living in the Midwest and I was working full-time in Texas as a high school guidance counselor. My parents were both educated and well-traveled people. Very social. They loved going out to dinner and to card parties. My mother had auburn hair and flashing green eyes and a sprinkle of freckles on the bridge of her nose. We used to laugh at all the lotions she used to try to hide those freckles. My mother loved to dress up. So did my father. He had an enormous tie collection and a closet full of nice suits. They talked to each other constantly. Well, my mother was actually the talkative one and my father liked to listen. They fought at times too but I never doubted their love. They believed in traditional values and were active in their church. I always thought of them as busy, interesting people.

But when my mom turned 70 her health started to disintegrate. She experienced a series of mini-strokes that left her progressively more and more confused and disoriented. Eventually she began to suffer from severe dementia and it got to the point where she could no longer even speak. The strokes slurred her speech so profoundly that I think she started to give up because no one could understand her. It was a terrible fate for my mother who was a brilliant and articulate woman. I remember how impatient my father would get with her faltering speech. She would work so hard to make herself understood and then rage at him when he tried to finish her sentences, especially when they were having conversations with other people. He was trying to help her but it was terribly frustrating for them both.

A big part of my mom's decline was depression. At the beginning of her dementia, she was aware that she was losing her faculties, losing her ability to communicate and as that got worse, her depression got worse and she finally gave up. She eventually stopped trying to communicate at all. I gave her pads of paper and for awhile she could write out her thoughts but soon even her writing became incoherent. Sometimes I could decipher a word or two and understand what she was trying to tell me but I could see the pain in her eyes, not physical pain, but the pain of losing that communication. It was horrible to see her falling away from the world that way.

I had always felt a special connection to my mom. Our relationship was different than her relationship with my sister. My mom and I were soul-mates. We thought alike. We looked alike. Right down to our freckles. For my whole life, no matter how far away I was, I'd suddenly have a feeling about my mom and sure enough, I'd call her up and we'd be thinking about the very same thing at the very same moment. We shared that kind of spiritual connection and when she fell apart physically and then mentally, I was devastated.

For the first few years of my mother's illness, my father cared for her during the school year and I spent summers taking care of them both. She was still well enough for my dad to put her in the car and drive her down to Houston to stay with us a couple times during the year. But as her condition worsened and she started having really bad spells, I'd have to hop on a plane and fly up for the weekend or take time off from school to help care for her.

Her deteriorating health impacted my dad's quality of life too. He was a wonderful caregiver but he was in tremendous denial about how bad my mom really was. He still wanted to take her out and have people over. I went crazy trying to care for them long distance. I'd hire people to come in and clean and cook for them and then find out weeks later that the people I'd hired had never shown up. My mom and dad wouldn't want to bother me but I'd call and find out that mother hadn't had a bath in a week. Their house wasn't handicapped accessible and they had an old-fashioned bathtub so she absolutely had to have help taking care of herself physically. I think that was something my father wasn't really comfortable helping her do. Then she started to become incontinent and began having those kinds of issues too.

During my visits, I'd fill their freezer with meals they could warm up, but even that started to become too much for my dad to handle. So I arranged for Meal on Wheels and that was OK for awhile but it wasn't the food they were used to. When I finally moved them to a care facility, most of the food I'd prepared was still sitting in their freezer. My dad said he just couldn't figure out how to deal with it.

Helping them make the decision to move out of their house wasn't easy and it ultimately wasn't really their decision. I planted those seeds for a long time. I'd say, "You guys really need to start thinking about moving" and they'd nod but that's about it. They didn't want to talk about it and they didn't want to go anywhere. They had lived in their house for 30 years and they were unwilling to acknowledge how bad the situation was becoming.

Moving them was my responsibility and mine alone. My sister was in Chicago and she helped a little but not much. She was also in denial because she didn't see mom and dad on a daily basis and she didn't know what was really going on. She wasn't very supportive but I decided she didn't get a vote on this because she wasn't the one doing the work. If you don't have someone's total support, it's easier to do it yourself in the way you want to do it and that's what I did.

I spent a whole summer looking at different facilities. My biggest dilemma was whether to put my parents together or to separate them.

They wanted to be together; my dad really made that clear. But my mom needed much more care than my father and assisted living is typically geared toward an individual. My dad needed independent living and my mom couldn't handle that. If they both went into assisted living I was afraid my dad's quality of life would go downhill.

I was specifically looking for good healthcare and the availability of a skilled nursing facility right on the premises because I knew my mom would eventually need that. I was also hoping to find a facility with a strong spiritual component but you end up having to weigh the priorities. I found a place with a spiritual component I liked, but the nursing care wasn't as good. Luckily I had a lot of support from my church and my neighbors. And some friends had also started the process of looking at facilities for their parents so we visited some of them together. That was helpful because we each thought of different questions to ask and then afterwards we compared notes.

Even though I did a lot of research into eldercare, I still came away feeling like I was forging my own path. I researched these facilities hoping to have my parents participate in the decision about where to move. I really wanted them to come with me to check out the different options. The ideal situation in my mind was to involve my parents in the decision-making while they still felt a sense of control. What was so hard was how quickly they felt like they had no control over their lives. You don't necessarily want to become the parent and make all the decisions for them as if they were children, but sometimes you're forced to. My parents just kept dragging their heels. They'd say, "No, we're happy where we are." And they wouldn't tell me about the problems they were having because they knew it meant having to once again hear my arguments for why they needed to move.

It was really my own breakdown that made the whole thing finally happen. I ended up moving them to a care facility when I realized I just couldn't physically handle their needs anymore. Nine years ago my husband was transferred to the Midwest, which was a blessing because we were able to move closer to my parents. As their needs increased I gave up more and more of my own time to care for them. At first I went down to visit them every couple of weeks and stayed two or three days. Then I started going every weekend but I quickly realized that they needed more care than I was able to give even going down two or three days a week. I was giving up my own life and wearing myself ragged. I felt like I was drowning. And I was physically not well. I was plagued by migraines brought on by all the stress. When I wasn't down there, I was worried sick that there was going to be a tremendous crisis with my mom. I just knew I couldn't go on like that.

I was at the breaking point and had to make a decision because nobody else was going to do it. So I finally said to them, "Look, you've got to help me out because I can't do this anymore. Enough is enough. You're not eating properly and mother's hygiene is the pits. Please help me find somewhere for you to go." Maybe they heard the desperation in my voice because they finally agreed to visit a couple of places I had found near my home. And when two rooms became available at The Village, my parents agreed to move there. They were never happy about moving but because I forced the issue, they agreed to do it.

That was five years ago. The Village is an assisted living facility with an attached nursing facility and an independent living center. At the time my dad didn't need assisted living but my mother definitely did. The Village fit our needs primarily because they had room for a couple. Most places just have one room because it's usually an individual who is trying to move into these facilities. The Village had two empty apartments right next each other and we created a door between them and turned one into my parents' living area and the other into their bedroom. It worked out great for about a year until my mother fell down and broke her hip. After that happened, they moved her to the nursing center.

Frankly, the nursing center wasn't great and I think my experience is a pretty common one. Patients are left too long without being checked on. Basic care is not wonderful. People are just parked and left. If you aren't an advocate for your loved one, they really do get shortchanged. Luckily, because the nursing center was attached to the rest of the complex, my dad was able to visit her several times a day and I was there at least once and sometimes twice a day. And I would go at different times so that they never knew when I was coming. My mother was a fastidious person and she cared deeply about her appearance. She had always been immaculately dressed so if I saw that she was unkempt or had something spilled on the front of her blouse, I'd make them change her. I wanted her to look nice. On Sundays, I wanted them to dress her up. She had always been such a fine lady, so we put pretty blouses on her and her necklaces. She loved her jewelry. I just wanted them to treat her with dignity in hopes that they might think about doing that with everybody else there too.

I definitely believe that grooming is critical to somebody's mental state and when hers wasn't up to par I'd say something. Of course you have to be careful not to be too pushy or grouchy about it. But I found a couple of people who were sympathetic and who liked my mom. One of the aides looked out for her and called me several times when she saw a problem. Other families would look out for each other's parents. I made a point of getting to know everyone she came in contact with including her caregivers, the woman who did the laundry and the cleaning people. You have to do what you have to do.

Although my mother spent a year in the nursing center before she died, I feel like I'd lost her a long, long time before. I'd been grieving such a long time for her. And she'd been grieving all those years as well. I was really just praying for her release. In her last year she was in such a bad way physically with a broken hip and all her other failing body parts. She had to suffer the indignity of diapers. She was absolutely miserable. She didn't need words to communicate that. She told me with her eyes.

During the last two months of her life she wouldn't even open her eyes and I knew she just wanted to go. How could I grieve at the very end when I knew that an end was all she prayed for? Finally she was released from a body that was doing her no good. She couldn't participate with life and the people she loved. When she finally died it was a relief. It was truly a blessing to say goodbye.

That was three years ago and since then my dad has been alone. He's 92 and he definitely needs assisted living now. He still rallies when he sees other people but he needs a lot of help with his medications. He's experiencing some mental deterioration but nothing like the dementia my mother suffered from. It's more a slow progression of old age and forgetfulness. His long-term memory is phenomenal but he can't remember what happened five minutes ago.

We talk a lot about the fact that he's lived longer than anybody else in his family and he's quite proud of his longevity. He's still perking along. He's only been in the hospital two times in his entire life. Once for a tonsillectomy and once for a hernia. He's basically very healthy and he has a wonderful outlook on life. He always says, "I have lived the best life and I have no regrets. I'm really very blessed." He really believes that. He's never been cantankerous so caregiving for him has been a real joy. He never makes me feel guilty; any guilt I have is my own. He'd like for me to come every day but he understands that I might sometimes miss a day during the week. I do visit him almost everyday and I eat lunch with him at least once every week. And then my husband and I go every Sunday after church and have lunch with him so he knows we'll have lunch with him twice each week. And then I bring him over to my house two nights each week for dinner to give him an outlet and a change of scenery.

The biggest change I've seen in him since mom died is that he's gone from being a very social person to more of a recluse. He doesn't seem to have the energy for anything more than a chat with me and then sitting in his La-Z-Boy and taking naps. I bring him the paper everyday but I'm not sure he reads it. He keeps the TV on but I don't think he absorbs it. He no longer goes to church with me and he likes to sleep until 11:00 each morning. I'm not sure if this is a natural slowing down or if the activities at the facility don't interest him. I can't say I blame him. The activities they offer aren't very creative.

These facilities can be terribly lonely places. Those of us who visit regularly end up adopting everybody on the floor. There are so many lonely people who just love to talk and often there's nobody there to listen. I think many of the aides and staff members see a bunch of people who are deteriorating and they don't realize that inside those poor bodies there are wonderful people just drying up. Articulate, interesting people with lives full of wisdom and adventures and nobody's reaching in and pulling this stuff out. Nobody's listening to all their incredible histories, thoughts and accomplishments.

It's the same with my dad. He still has so many great stories to tell. Not about yesterday or five minutes ago, but about his life 50 or 75 years ago. Stories about my mother and his time in the war. About growing up on the farm and being the first in his family to attend school. It's so heartbreaking that my mom couldn't say a single word at the end of her life, and all my dad wants to do is talk. So I make sure to listen. He talks about the journey of his life and in his journey I keep finding lessons for my own. I love my dad very much. Before he falls away from the world like my mom, I want to make sure that I'm there to hear everything he wants to tell me. I know that soon enough I'll be walking down that long and winding road alone.

Senior Housing Options

Independent Living (retirement) Community

...is for people with limited medical problems, who can maintain their own living area and attend to own care. No custodial or medical care is provided as part of the rent. If health declines, separate arrangements have to be made to provide care. Retirement communities consist of fully equipped private apartments with rent from $1000 to $2500 a month. Most are private pay, Medicare does not cover. The communities often have organized social activities.

Assisted Living

...is for people who can no longer live on own safely, but do not require nursing home. They consist of small apartments, usually efficiencies, often for a single person. Assisted living provides activities, social interaction, group meals, as well as assistance with medications, acts of daily living, housekeeping, monitoring, and supervision. Rent is $1800-$3500 per month for a single and $2800-3800 per month with a spouse. Most are private pay, but some accept Medicare.

Nursing Home

...is for people who need 24 hour skilled nursing and custodial care. Price ranges from $4000 to $8000 a month. Most nursing homes are at least partially covered by Medicare or Medicaid, with some private pay.

Continuing Care Retirement Community

...is a combination of all three. It provides continuous care from independent living all the way through skilled nursing for entire life of the resident. Continuing care is beneficial because as a person's health deteriorates, she stays in the same facility. Some continuing care facilities require that residents start in the independent living section first, so parents who are in need of assisted living straight from living at home may not qualify.

Home Care

…is staying in one's own home while receiving some assistance. Paid assistance is available from a few hours to entire 24 hour care. Medicare and Medicaid cover some parts of home care. Home health aides or nurses are usually paid by the hour or day: Home Health Aide $20+/hour and Skilled Nursing - $400+/day.

Questions to ask if hiring in help:

 • What services are needed?
 • Will the same home health professional provide care?
 • How long has the service been in business? (And ask for references)
 • Does Provider do background checks, bonding, training classes?

If starting home care, be present during the first several aide visits.

Meals on Wheels © is a community based program which delivers meals to home-bound people. Fees are on a sliding scale. See Website Appendix for contact information.

Choosing the Right Place

Be proactive and research facilities BEFORE your parent needs help. Many admissions follow a hospital stay where you might get a 24-hour notice that a move is necessary.

Questions to ask yourself, staff, and residents at the housing facility:

+ Are the residents clean and properly dressed?
+ Does the staff respond quickly to calls for help?
+ Does the staff seem comfortable with each other and residents?
+ Do the residents have the same caregivers on a daily basis?
+ What is the staffing ratio? What about weekends?
+ How frequent is the turnover of staff?
+ Are there social workers, therapists and activity directors on staff?
+ Are there family events?

Making the Move

Moving an elderly parent into a senior living facility is an act of love, not a denial of duty. Many older adults flourish with the new friends, activities and experiences and become reconnected, more physical, social and verbal. Their health improves with the regular medical care and a consistent meal program. Boredom and depression are decreased.

Getting Mom to Move

Know her passions and hobbies
Talk with others who have made the move
Enlist an advocate: doctor, minister, grandchild, friend
Stay positive
Don't give up
Be prepared with options before you start the discussion

When talking to Mom:

+ Focus on the good reasons to move, not the negative reasons for staying in her home
+ Focus on the quality of life
+ Senior communities provide more social interaction than the adult child can provide

+ Use someone else as an example of a positive move
+ Express your concern for safety, security, peace of mind
+ You want to know her wishes BEFORE a crisis
+ Talk about your needs, crying is okay
+ Therapeutic fibbing: sometimes lying is okay. An example: tell her the move will be cost effective because it will be paid by Medicare

Try a short-term stay (respite) for 1 month to get acclimated.

Making the move more positive

Give new mailing address to old friends

Have her minister visit

Bring favorite foods when visiting

Take walks around the facility to meet new people and familiarize with facility

Decorate her room for the holidays

Eat meals with her in the dining room

Have the grandchildren's groups come perform

Visit during quiet times in the schedule to provide a diversion

Attend scheduled activities with parent

Visit at random hours

Talk with residents and their families

Befriend a staff person. Hang out

Bring the staff doughnuts!

God's Timetable

Amelia's Story

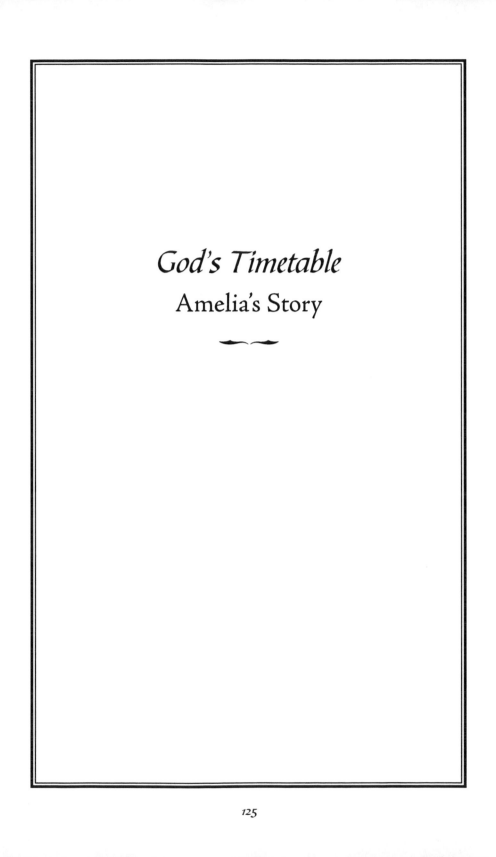

My first home was in your womb
Thank you for the lovely room
My next home was your home too
And you shared with me, you cared for me
Like only a mama can do

No ocean floor lies deeper
No perfume is sweeter
And no gift is given freer
Than a mother's love

My first steps were at your side
Each success fed by your pride
You've always held out a loving hand
And you hold me, enfold me
Like only a mama can

I know sometimes I drive you crazy
Sometimes you drive me there, too
But the ties are strong so it don't take long
'Til the love comes pourin' through

"A Mother's Love"
By Karen Taylor-Good

God's Timetable

When Momma died, my brothers and sisters and I didn't feel scared or sad because we knew she was going home to the Lord. We're Christians, and for a Christian what's better than death? Of course we grieved the whole time Momma was ill, but her death wasn't unexpected or even unwelcome. Also, my four siblings and I experienced a lot of death growing up. Our grandmother, father, aunt, uncle and cousins all died while we were young so we already knew death was a part of life. Momma and Daddy always said that we live and die on God's timetable. Only God knows why he took Daddy so soon and let Momma stay down here with us. We just feel blessed that we had her as long as we did.

Momma and Daddy's marriage was a little bit unusual. They got married when she was 26 and he was 42 and they had five kids spread out over 14 years. Daddy had been Momma's music teacher. He was a professional musician and was very accomplished for a person of color in that era. He graduated from Julliard in New York and worked with some of the most celebrated musicians of the day. When he moved back to the Midwest, he married Momma. They were both devout Christians. Neither drank or smoked but they had a vibrant social life and a very interesting circle of friends and artists.

Of course, we always had the most wonderful music in our house. Evenings were filled with laughter, music, food, and exciting energy. All of us kids were busy with cultural activities, art lessons, dance classes, music lessons and a lot of socializing. Momma and Daddy had a vision of what they wanted for us. College, cultural achievement and Christian values. Even after Daddy died Momma stuck to that vision for us and made sure it happened.

We all attended an academically demanding magnet school and our parents were sticklers for grades. Especially Momma. She whipped us if we got bad grades. She and Daddy believed that whipping instilled discipline and respect. I remember a time soon after Daddy had his first heart attack. He was resting upstairs while my brother Jeremiah and I were downstairs washing the dishes. Jeremiah had gotten a swat at school for calling the teacher a "fat pig" and while he and I were washing dishes the phone rang. All I remember was Momma getting off the phone and saying, "Jeremiah, we're going down to the basement." The whipping he got in the basement with a strap was the worst one I ever remember him getting. Momma and Daddy taught us that disrespect and talking back were unacceptable and I'm pretty sure that was the last time Jeremiah ever got in trouble at school.

Daddy was an emotional person but Momma wasn't at all. He liked to hug and kiss us but Momma never did. She just wasn't a touchy-feely sort of person. She was a perfectionist and very strict about how we looked, spoke and acted. She carried herself with style and wanted us to do the same. We thought Momma was beautiful but for some reason she considered herself ugly. She thought her sisters were the beautiful ones. Momma was Black but she was so fair that she easily passed for White. She had blue eyes and natural platinum blonde hair that was so unusual that people would walk up and touch it. She had a slim, beautiful body and she worked hard to maintain it even after having five children. She sewed beautiful clothes that accentuated her figure and we were always proud of her. It's strange that she never considered herself pretty.

Both Momma and Daddy were active in the Republican Party. Momma in particular was something of a political activist. She was a champion for kids, especially black kids, and she was very concerned with inequality in education. She was extremely complex and a very honest person. Because of that a lot of people thought she was mean, but actually she was just a straight shooter. She didn't tolerate foolishness, shady characters, fudging or anything that wasn't clean. She was discerning. She had a sense that right was right and wrong was wrong.

The Lord decided to take Daddy home when my oldest brother was 16, my youngest brother was 2 and I was about 12. After Daddy died, we kids raised little Miles because Momma started working full-time. While Daddy was alive, Momma had mostly been a stay-at-home mom who worked every once in a while as a tax examiner. When Daddy died, Momma started working full-time for the IRS and little Miles went everywhere with us. We treated him like he was our pet.

Momma came from a large family and she had already taught us kids to do chores around the house, so after Daddy died the house worked pretty well despite her being gone so much. We all cooked, cleaned, ironed and kept things on track because Momma did not tolerate disorganization or messiness. We had to straighten up the house everyday so that when she got home from work the house was clean and dinner was ready. We also had someone who came in to help clean and care for us.

Momma liked nice things so we had a lot of nice things growing up. She loved fine fabrics and trims and somehow she found time to upholster our furniture and sew all our clothes so that each piece was an incredible work of art. All our friends would hang out at our house because the refrigerator was always full and Momma liked having people in the house. So even though Daddy died when we were all so young, our childhood was actually pretty wonderful.

When Momma got to be about 68 or 69, she started having health problems. We older kids had been out of the house for years by then and Miles was in college. Momma woke up one morning with an excruciating stomachache. We drove her to the hospital and it turned out to be diverticulitis. She had to have emergency surgery and her recovery took a long time. She was in the hospital for weeks and had to have a colostomy. After being released from the hospital, she came to my house to recuperate for another three months. I didn't have any kids yet and my oldest brother lived nearby so we took care of Momma's dressings and colostomy bag together. After she recuperated, she moved back home and retired from the IRS. She recovered well enough that she eventually took a part-time job with the EPA for a couple years and lived independently just fine. When she wasn't working, she was shopping. Momma just loved to shop. She collected china, glassware, cut crystal, oriental rugs, fabrics and silverware. She was also very generous. Momma gave away even more than she collected.

When Momma turned 72, she developed heart problems and had open-heart surgery. At the time she was healthy except for mild diabetes, but she ended up with complications from the heart surgery and was in the hospital for about three months. The doctors told us that one of the side effects of surgery in older people was the onset of dementia from the anesthesia. That really happened to Momma. Dementia got a foothold and Momma became extremely disoriented in the hospital. There were days she didn't know where she was or who we were, but her disorientation lessened over time.

During that period my older brother and I put our names on her financial accounts so we could take care of her bills. Ultimately we decided to shift the responsibility for all of her care over to us and she willingly signed over those responsibilities. After she got out of the hospital she came to my house again for a month and then she went back home and lived by herself with our help for another couple of years. My oldest brother and I would check on her every day. I would go during the afternoon and cook her meals or bring over leftovers. I would make sure she'd taken all her insulin and medications. My brother would check on her in the evening to make sure she'd eaten her dinner and had taken her medication. Her dementia was not severe during this period so she was pretty lucid and her diabetes was still on the mild side.

Momma lived on her own pretty well. I bought her groceries and she got up each morning to fix her own breakfast. We got her a microwave so she could heat food up easily. She was definitely in the first stages of dementia so I ordered her medicines and paid all her bills because those were the sorts of details she couldn't pay attention to. I really didn't mind doing this for her and my husband was very supportive. Momma had watched our two kids for us in the past so it just felt like it was our turn to help her. Of course there were a few times it felt onerous. Like when my kids had something going on and I had to balance getting to Momma and dealing with other things, but usually I could stop by her house without a problem. The truth is I enjoyed being with her. We watched soap operas and talked. She showed me things she'd bought in the past and I helped her clean. It didn't feel like a heavy burden.

We kids were brought up being of service to others so caring for Momma felt like a natural thing to do. We tag-teamed: my brother, my cousin and I. My mother's family had done the same for their mother and we knew that's what you did. Kinship was really stressed in our family. Our cousins would come and check on Momma too. It just didn't seem unusual.

Well, Momma's independence came to an abrupt end one weekend when Miles was visiting and she went into congestive heart failure. We called 911 and in the hospital they told us her kidneys were failing too. All the siblings came to the hospital and the doctors told us we had a choice. Let her die or try dialysis. Let her die? She was our Momma. But we didn't want her suffering either. We knew that whatever decision we made would affect everyone's life, not just Momma's. So we went with our hearts and decided to have her try dialysis. We siblings worked out a schedule of someone getting her to and from dialysis three times a week so that she would have familiar faces around her at all times. This coincided with her dementia getting worse and we decided that checking in on her twice a day was not enough. We were especially concerned about her being alone at night and perhaps starting to wander or having another health episode.

The only person in the family who was in a position to easily move in was Miles who had just finished college. So we asked him to move back home so he could be with Momma at night. He agreed and we hired a health aide to come several mornings a week and a housekeeper to be with Momma when Miles was at work. We also all checked on her every day and helped each other so no one had to shoulder the burden alone.

I still did her cooking because I knew what she liked and things went on like that for quite awhile.

Miles was great. He was able to say things to Momma the rest of us couldn't because he was the baby and he and Momma had a special bond. He was like an only child since he was so much younger than the rest of us. Not all of the siblings understood the severity of the situation but Miles really got it. He monitored her carefully and stayed with her nearly every night. He gave up much of his social life but he seemed to be OK with that. Also, each of us took Momma into our homes for a weekend to give Miles a break. But Miles had her most evenings and we were thankful that he was willing to do it.

After a few years of this, Momma got very sick. She'd had a variety of infections with the dialysis but she always pulled through. She'd go to the hospital for four or five days and then she'd bounce back and we'd bring her home. After one of these episodes with her in the hospital, Miles finally said he couldn't do it anymore. The emergency trips to the hospital at 3 a.m. were getting to be too much. He was tired of being there every evening and her dementia was getting worse. We had locks and alarms on every door so she wouldn't wander and it was difficult for Miles. He couldn't sleep well because he was always listening for one of the alarms to go off.

The social worker at the hospital suggested we put her in a nursing home. We knew it would be easier to put her in a nursing home directly from the hospital so my older brother and I started looking at places. We looked at a lot of places and most of them were incredibly depressing. Momma had a decent income from daddy's retirement and her federal pension. She was comfortable and the house was paid off so she could afford whatever she needed. She had excellent medical insurance so there were few of those bills. We planned to turn all her money over to the nursing home and have the rest of her care covered by Medicaid. We were looking for a bed that would be reimbursed by Medicaid but not all nursing home facilities have those beds available because of the amount of red tape involved in dealing with the Medicaid program.

After a long and terribly frustrating search, we walked into a facility that immediately looked and felt like Momma's house. It had similar furniture to hers, it was pleasant and it was only seven minutes from my house. And they had a Medicaid bed! We talked to the director and I was honest with him about how severe Momma's dementia was by then. The director just patted my arm and said, "They all get to be that way eventually. It's going to be OK." I looked at my brother and said, "God just lead us here. I literally felt His hand."

We visited Momma everyday, which was absolutely critical. I don't care how good the place is or how expensive it is; you've just got to be there. Just to make sure things are going OK. I continued to do her laundry and, for the first year, we still took her to dialysis three days a week. We still wanted to have familiar faces around her whenever possible.

While she was in the nursing home she continued to have problems with infections from the dialysis. Several times we thought her time had come and we all gathered at the hospital to be with her at the end. But she'd bounce back again and go back to the nursing home. For us, the grieving went on while Momma was slowly dying from her illness, not after she passed away. It was hard to watch her gradually fading away, growing more frail and confused. Being in the hospital was really tough on her. And it was tough on us too. It was so important to us during this emotional time to have family there to laugh and reflect with. Family and the Lord. I don't know what we would have done without those two things. We all gathered at Momma's bedside laughing and talking. Not that we didn't understand the gravity of her situation, but dealing with her death was a part of our lives. Yes, it was an imposition at times, but it was part of who we were and we accepted the burden.

After a few of these infections, Momma was in a weakened state but she was still active and knew who we were. She mostly sat around at the nursing home, but she had good roommates and they connected with her. They would tell us all about her and her day. And we'd drop in at all hours. Literally. Just to check. To see what was going on.

The following Christmas Eve she ended up back in the hospital and the doctor came by when we were all standing around her bed. He took a look at her and said, "She has no quality of life." She did bounce back one last time and she returned to the nursing home, but her appetite started dwindling and she was in the end stages of dementia. She could still recognize us and she could talk a bit but she was really coming to the end. About a week before she died, on a Sunday night, she was getting ready for bed and we had a pretty good conversation but by the next evening she had stopped talking. Her kidneys shut down completely and she went back to the hospital and really didn't talk again before she died a few days later.

My siblings and I were certainly not angels or martyrs. There were many times I felt tired and I was thinking, "Jeez, I don't feel like going to see Momma." But that's just what you do. We had good support from our spouses. My husband never once said, "You're going to visit her again?" I put 75,000 miles on our car in three years going to see Momma. My brothers' spouses never complained and even offered to have Momma come live with them.

I suppose everyone wonders if they could have done more or made a different decision about a parent's care. But I believe everything happens for a reason and that God is in control of all this. The key is to do whatever it takes to honor your parents. We were trying to make a decision about whether to continue Momma's dialysis and a nurse said to me, "Do the right thing for your mother because these doctors don't really care. They'll tell you to do something on Saturday and on Monday they've completely forgotten about it. But you'll live with it the rest of your life." The right decision is the right decision before the Lord. God takes people through the dying process for a reason. We, the survivors, want to comfort ourselves by not seeing our parents suffer. For that reason we are tempted to bring things to an end before the natural dying process would allow, but that's not our realm.

My siblings and I never considered hurrying our mother's death for our own comfort. We didn't do anything overly invasive or unnecessary for Momma, but we did things to keep her here. And God honored that.

We felt an essence of Momma right up to the very end. Before Momma went to the hospital for the last time, she was sitting in the activity room in the nursing home and we were trying to get her to eat some dinner. Now her favorite thing in the world was ice cream and the staff would use ice cream as a bribe to get her to cooperate. So I said, "Momma, if you eat your dinner, I'll get you some of your favorite ice cream." And she looked up at me and in her quiet, raspy voice she slowly and distinctly said, "Let me see the ice cream first." No duping her right up to the end. We all started laughing: Momma, me and the staff.

It would be so sad to live with regret or guilt for the rest of our lives. None of us have any regrets about what we did for Momma. We have wonderful memories and no regrets. We loved Momma but we weren't necessarily sad at the end. The end was peaceful. When she was still living in her house she told me, "I'm not going to be around here that much longer but I'm not afraid to die because I'm a Christian."

Our brother's wife was admitted to the hospital several years after Momma died and she happened to be on the same floor that Momma had been on and the same nurses were there. One day they were looking at her chart and noticed her last name, which is an unusual spelling. They told her that there'd been a woman in the hospital with the same last name who'd had one of the strongest family bonds they'd ever seen. They were talking about us.

The truth is the medical community was ready to let Momma go long before we were. All I can say is don't make a decision that you won't be able to live with based on someone else's advice. You know whether your parents are fighters or whether they want to give up. And don't be afraid to let them go. We weren't ready to let Momma go until she made it clear she was tired and prepared to go home to be with the Lord. And over time we got ready to let her go. We were blessed with having Christian parents and we were at peace letting both of them go. Thanks to them we had that foundation and that faith in God's timetable.

Aging Well

Most adult children are working at implementing anti-aging science into their daily routine. Being healthy and vital is a priority. Baby Boomers never expect to age! A study done in the 1970's tested people in Georgia who were 100 years old. After much medical and psychological testing, Four factors were common to all the participants. 1) They all had a passion for something. 2) They tested optimistic on standardized tests. 3) They had developed coping mechanism for dealing with death. 4) They had a belief in a higher being.

Now there are new studies that have expanded those indicators.

Living a longer and happier life:

Be active: exercise

Express gratitude and joy

Forgive: let go of anger and resentments

Display integrity

Be passionate: engage in life

Good nutrition and weight management

Relationships: have at least one good friend

Be a life long learner: keep mentally active

Keep the emphasis on growing: not growing older

Develop a healthy coping mechanism: cope well with loss

Maintain a faith in a higher being

Be optimistic

Laugh a lot

Have age-appropriate doctor visits and tests

No smoking and limited alcohol

Make good choices: wear seat belts, sunscreen/hat/sunglasses, helmets.
Brush teeth, floss.

Statistics:

Up to age 65 – 70% of how we age and our health is controlled by
individual life choices

After age 65 – 90% of how we age and our health is controlled by
individual life choices

A survey of 85+ year olds asked, "What would you have done
differently?"

The answers: I would have left more than a financial legacy to others,
and I would have taken more risks and taken the road less traveled.

Appendix A:
THE LIST

When it is my turn to be taken care of...
I WILL

Do something for my mind, body, spirit.

Say "I'll try," instead of "I can't."

Keep thinking.

Find and support a positive cause.

Do something philanthropic.

Have a hobby or passion.

Leave the house every day to do something.

Be a life long learner.

Be clean and take pride in how I look.

Keep my body moving.

Stand upright and straight: keep head position up.

Get dressed! Update look: hair, dress, eyeglasses.

Update house. Keep clean and sorted.

Hire out things to be done, so my kids don't have to do the work.

Move to appropriate housing.

Give away things during my lifetime.

Flush the toilet.

Be thankful and appreciative.

Listen to suggestions of friends and family.

Try new things.

Be social.

Have and be fun: have sense of humor about growing older.

Push myself out of my comfort zone every day.

Be kind.

Smell the roses.

Be positive.

Make and keep friends.

Talk about what I DO, not about my problems.

Be joyful.

Be responsible for my actions. Not a victim.

Say, "I'm sorry". Make things right today!

Be open. Trust.
Be flexible.
Stop driving when my children ask me to.
Listen to my children.
Get finances and legal papers done.
Keep current.
Treat all my children equally.
Make happy family memories.
Take my whole family on a great vacation.
Pass out hugs.
Play.

I WON'T

Moan and groan.
Be bossy or rude.
Keep track of all the negatives or hold grudges.
Get paranoid.
Cry and weep continually.
Say, "I wish I were dead."
Say, "Now I am ALL alone" to the caretaker who is standing by my
    side!
Drink alcohol.
Criticize.

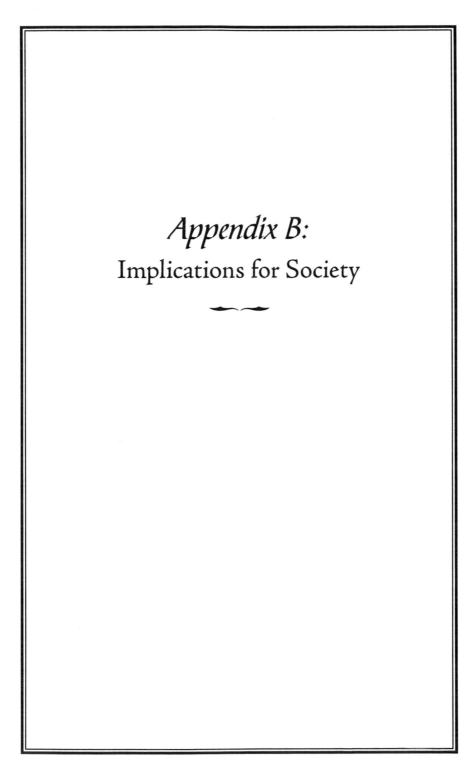

Appendix B:
Implications for Society

The costs and time of caregiving will impact government and personal resources in ways that are just now immerging. Over 55 million adult children are now caregiving elderly relatives, thus placing unanticipated financial pressure on these Boomers. There is even a new label for these caregivers who are *Stuck in the Middle* – the "60-year-old kid" (Neal Cutler, financial gerontologist).

Family caregivers save society billions of dollars each year. With the elderly now being the fastest growing segment of the population, programs to meet the needs of the elderly will have to expand and consume more of the gross national product.

STATISTICS

+ Currently only 2% of the National Institutes of Health budget is devoted to Alzheimer research.
+ 1 in 8 people over the age of 65 have Alzheimer's Disease.
+ Alzheimer's is the seventh leading cause of death.

The average caregiver of the elderly is…
46-57 years old
Female (3/5 of caregivers)
Married
Employed
Some college education
Provide 20+ hours per week of caregiving

¼ of the population is caregiving the elderly
2/3 of caregivers are employed outside the home
84% have made adjustments to work-life in order to caregive
21% of employers offer eldercare benefits
80% of home care services are provided by family caregivers
50% of nursing home expenses are paid directly by the elderly or their families
$400-700 out-of-pocket paid monthly by the adult child
Adult child will devote 10-15 years caregiving their elderly parents

Appendix C:
Resources/websites

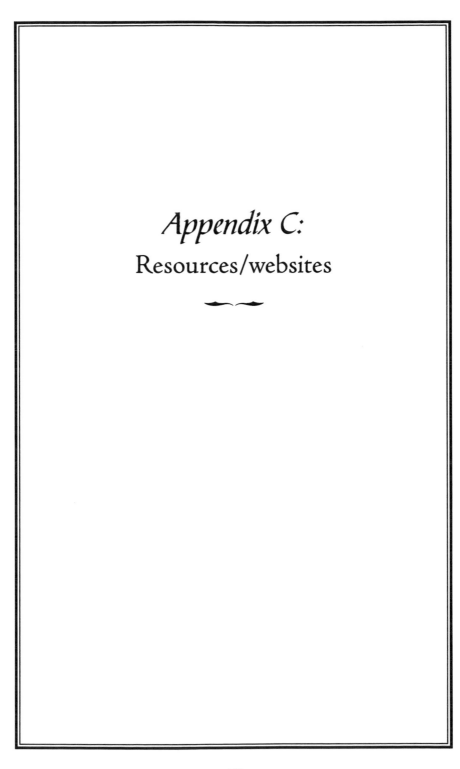

Many wonderful informational sites exist. The following listing is a sample of what is available on the internet and does not denote any endorsement on the part of the author.

Caregiving Stories
www.CaregivingStories.com
Shared stories and tips for caregiving your elderly parents
More information on *Stuck in the Middle*

Barbara McVicker
www.BarbaraMcVicker.com
Information about the author and her services as a speaker and
    consultant

AGING

Alliance for Aging Research
1-202-293-2856
www.agingresearch.org
Non-profit supporting discoveries to improve aging and health

American Society on Aging
1-800-537-9728
www.asaging.org
Largest organization of professionals in the field of aging

Children of Aging Parents
1-800-227-7294
www.caps4caregivers.org
Provides information, referrals, and support

Eldercare Locator: Department of Health and Human Services
1-800-677-1116
www.eldercare.gov
Nationwide directory assistance for eldercare

National Association of Area Agencies on Aging

1-202-872-0888

www.n4a.org

Locate your local Area Agency on Aging

National Council on Aging

1-202-479-1200

www.ncoa.org

Resources on health, staying independent, and volunteering

National Institute on Aging

1-800-222-2225

www.nia.nih.gov

Information and research about health and aging

HEALTHCARE

Alzheimer's Association

1-800-272-3900

www.alz.org

Learn about diagnosis, treatments, and clinical trials

www.alz.org/we_can_help_safe_return.asp

Safe Return© program

Alzheimer's Disease Education & Referral Center (National Institute on Aging)
1-800-438-4380
www.alzheimers.org
Information on diagnosis, treatment, caregiving, and long-term care

American Cancer Society
1-800-ACS-2345
1-800-227-2345
www.cancer.org
Information about cancer, treatment, and caregiving

American Heart Association
1-800-AHA-USA-1
1-800-242-8721
www.amhrt.org
Information about heart attack, stroke, and other heart diseases

American Occupational Therapy Association
1-301-652-2682
www.aota.org
Information about occupational therapy and referrals to find a therapist

American Parkinson Disease Association
1-800-223-2732
www.apdaparkinson.org
Information on Parkinson's including caregiver support

American Stroke Association
1-888-478-7653
www.strokeassociation.org
Information on the warning signs of stroke and life after stroke

Arthritis Foundation
1-800-283-7800
www.arthritis.org
Provides disease and self-help information

Medicare
1-800-MEDICARE
1-800-633-4227
www.medicare.gov
Information about Medicare services

National Association of Professional Geriatric Care Managers
1-520-881-8008
www.caremanager.org
Referral listing

National Institute of Health: Senior Health
www.nihseniorhealth.gov
Features popular health topics for older adults

Society for Vascular Surgery
1-877-282-2010
www.vascularweb.org
Information about free screening

Visiting Nurse Associations of America
1-617-737-3200
www.vnaa.org
Information about in-home nursing

MENTAL HEALTH

Helpguide

www.helpguide.org

Non-commercial information on mental health and life-long wellness

Links to assessment questions

National Alliance on Mental Illness

1-800-950-6264

www.nami.org

Information on many different mental illnesses, especially depression

National Institute of Mental Health

www.nimh.nih.gov

Answers to all kinds of mental health questions

END OF LIFE

Aging with Dignity

1-888-594-7437

www.agingwithdignity.org

Developed "Five Wishes" to assist families in discussing end-of-life issues

Caring Connections
1-800-989-9455
www.partnershipforcaring.org
Dying and end-of-life resources including advance directives for every state
Free downloads of Medial Power of Attorney

Growth House
www.growthhouse.org
Provides information about terminal illness and Hospice

Hard Choices for Loving People
From A&A Publishers
www.hardchoices.com
The best pamphlet to help make difficult end of life choices

Hospice Foundation of America
1-800-854-3402
www.hospicefoundation.org
Hospice care improves the quality of a patient's last days by offering comfort and dignity.

CONSUMER AND LEGAL PROTECTION

American Bar Association: Commission on Law and Aging
1-202-662-8690
www.abanet.org/aging
Help with legal issues

National Reverse Mortgage Lenders Association
www.reversemortgage.org
The latest information on reverse mortgage options

National Senior Citizens Law Center
1-202-289-6976
www.nsclc.org
Advocates for elderly on issues of income and health

USA.gov: Government made easy
1-800-FED-INFO
1-800-333-4636
www.seniors.gov
Federal and State aging websites
Health, education, laws, consumer information with many facts and
    links

OTHER

American Association of Homes and Services for the Aging
1-202-783-2242
www.aahsa.org
Help for housing options

American Association of Retired Persons (AARP)
1-888-687-2277
www.aarp.org
Advocacy and information for people over 50

American Red Cross
1-800-RED-CROSS
1-800-733-2767
www.redcross.org
Offers courses on caregiving

Elderhostel
1-800-454-5768
www.elderhostel.org
Life-long learning available around the world

Meals on Wheels Association of America
1-703-548-5558
www.mowaa.org
Delivers hot food to elderly

National Safety Council
1-800-621-6244
Information about a refresher course for car driving

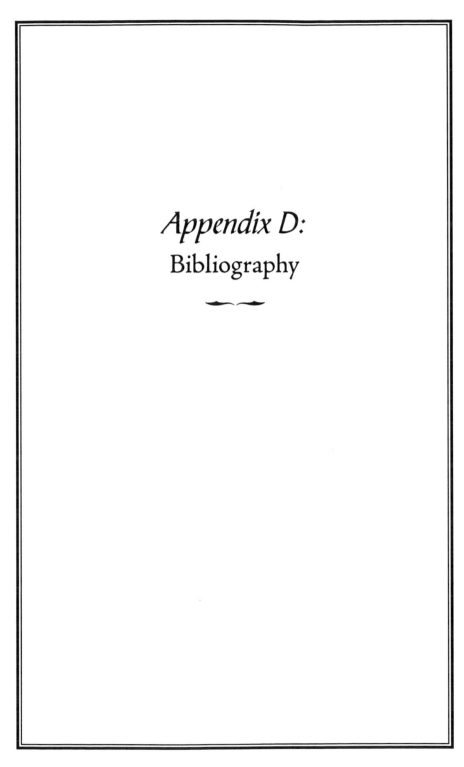

Appendix D:
Bibliography

Beerman, Susan and Judith Rappaport-Mission. *Eldercare 911: the Caregiver's Complete Handbook for Making Decisions.* Prometheus Books, 2002.

Brickey, Michael, Ph.D. *Defy Aging: Develop the Mental and Emotional Vitality to Live Longer, Healthier, and Happier Than You Ever Imagined.* New Resources Press, 2000.

Carr, Sasha and Sandra Choron. *Caregiver's Essential Handbook: More than 1,200 Tips to Help You Care for and Comfort the Seniors in Your Life.* McGraw-Hill. 2003.

Delehanty, Hugh and Elinor Ginzler. *Caring for Your Parents: The Complete AARP Guide.* Sterling Publishing. 2006.

Driscoll, Marilee. *The Complete Idiot's Guide to Long-term Care Planning.* Alpha, 2002.

Dunn, Hank. *Hard Choices for Loving People: CPR, Artificial Feeding, Comfort Care and the Patient with a Life-Threatening Illness.* A & A Publishers, Inc. 2001.
Available as a free pdf at www.hardchoices.com

Gruetzner, Howard, M.Ed. *Alzheimer's: A Caregiver's Guide and Sourcebook.* John Wiley & Sons, Inc., 2001.

Karpinski, Marion, RN. *Quick Tips for Caregivers.* Healing Arts Communications, 2000.

McLeod, Beth Witrogen, ed. *And Thou Shalt Honor: the Caregiver's Companion.* Rodale Books, 2003.

MetLife Consumer Education Center. "Caring for an Aging Loved One." 2006

Morris, Virginia and Robert Butler. *How to Care for Aging Parents.* NY: Workman Publishing, 2005.

Rust, Mike. *Taking Care of Mom and Dad: The Mechanics of Supporting Your Parents in Their Times of Need.* Silver Lake Publishing, 2001.

Satow, Roberta, PhD. *Doing the Right Thing: Taking Care of Your Elderly Parents Even if They Didn't Take Care of You.* Penguin, 2005.

Segrest, Melissa, ed. *Caregiving in the US.* National Alliance for Caregiving, 2005.

BARBARA MCVICKER

Author – Author of *Stuck in the Middle: Shared Stories and Tips for Caregiving Your Elderly Parents*, Barbara McVicker has written a book every adult child should purchase before beginning the challenging job of caring for aging parents. An essential overview of the most important proactive aspects of caregiving, this book is also the handbook for the "Sandwich Generation" when putting their own affairs in order.

Speaker – An educator and storyteller, Barbara McVicker speaks on many aspects of elder caregiving. Whether it's a keynote address for a national conference, or a workshop for corporate employees struggling to balance caregiving and career, Barbara offers practical insight to caregiving presented in an interactive and entertaining way.

Consultant – As a consultant, Barbara McVicker helps organizations support employees who are committed to caregiving their parents while maintaining their careers. Offering a variety of flexible formats, including employee education sessions and panel discussions, Barbara shares practical solutions for employees balancing caregiving and career.

Darby McVicker – Barbara's daughter and co-author of *Stuck in the Middle*, Darby McVicker was caregiver to her grandmother-in-law, who battled bone cancer. A director of religious education, Darby lives in Madison, Wisconsin, with her husband and son.

To Order Books:

Stuck in the Middle is available from most on-line and brick and mortar booksellers, including Amazon.com, Barnes & Noble, and Author House Publishing.
www.authorhouse.com/BookStore 1-888-519-5121

To Order CD's of Karen Taylor Good's songs: *www.karentaylorgood.com*

To Contact Barbara McVicker:
www.BarbaraMcVicker.com or *www.CaregivingStories.com*

Printed in the United States
201867BV00002B/1-105/P